SWARAJ

ARVIND KEJRIWAL is a social activist fighting to change the political system by bringing in transparency and people's participation. He is the main architect of the Anna Hazare-led anti-corruption agitation that shook the nation in 2011–12.

After graduating in mechanical engineering from IIT Kharagpur in 1989, Kejriwal joined Tata Steel. In 1992, he joined the India Revenue Service (IRS), and was joint commissioner in the income tax department. He took long leave from the government in 2000 to set up an NGO, Parivartan. Through this he worked for many years to change the lives of Delhi's slum dwellers, and was also active in the campaign for Right to Information (RTI). In 2006, he resigned from government service.

He was awarded the Ramon Magsaysay Award in 2006 for his work on RTI.

D1555317

SWARAJ

Arvind Kejriwal

HarperCollins *Publishers* India

First published in India in 2012 by
HarperCollins *Publishers* India

Copyright © Arvind Kejriwal 2012

ISBN: 978-93-5029-544-1

4 6 8 10 9 7 5 3

Arvind Kejriwal asserts the moral right to be identified as
the author of this work.

The views and opinions expressed in this book are the author's own
and the facts are as reported by him, and the publishers are not in any way
liable for the same.

HarperCollins *Publishers*
A-53, Sector 57, Noida 201301, India
77–85 Fulham Palace Road, London W6 8JB, United Kingdom
Hazelton Lanes, 55 Avenue Road, Suite 2900, Toronto, Ontario M5R 3L2
and 1995 Markham Road, Scarborough, Ontario M1B 5M8, Canada
25 Ryde Road, Pymble, Sydney, NSW 2073, Australia
31 View Road, Glenfield, Auckland 10, New Zealand
10 East 53rd Street, New York NY 10022, USA

Typeset in 12/15 Bembo Roman at
SÜRYA

Printed and bound at
Thomson Press (India) Ltd.

*For the common people of India who have been
waiting for swaraj*

CONTENTS

WHEN THE PEOPLE WILL DECIDE   **85**

BASELESS FEARS AND MISCONCEPTIONS   **93**

LET THERE BE A LAW FOR SELF-RULE   **109**

FOREWORD

There is a wave of change in the entire country today. Whatever be the religion, caste, creed, or age of a person, whether he is rich or poor, a city dweller or a villager, everyone seems to be dreaming about change. If this enthusiasm keeps up, something that has not happened in sixty-four years in India's history will happen in ten. But at this point in time it is very important for us to understand our future course of action. This opportunity should not get lost in an insignificant target such as a mere change of government. It is, therefore, very important to understand where we should now be headed.

Gandhiji used to say, 'True democracy is not run by twenty people sitting in Delhi. The power centres now are in capital cities like Delhi, Mumbai and Kolkata. I would like to distribute these power centres in seven lakh villages of India.' We celebrated our first Republic Day on 26 January 1950 but we forgot these words by Gandhiji. And that is why such a gulf between the rich and the poor exists today. There is an ever-growing rift between religions and castes. Corruption and the escalating cost of living is making life difficult for the common man. Even after sixty-four years of independence, there are hungry and unemployed people.

If we want to change the economy of the country, we have to change that of the villages. The economy cannot be changed by sitting in Delhi and formulating schemes or dispensing money through these schemes. This can only happen by empowering people. In our democracy today, the system is stronger than the people. It often seems that the system is far more valuable than the people it is meant for. We have to understand the meaning of true democracy. We have to understand that people's role in a democracy is not merely voting once every five years. They have to participate in governance. Power centres have to move from Delhi and other state capitals to villages and communities.

It is noteworthy that wherever gram sabhas (village councils) have taken shape, the village has seen tremendous development in just a few years. We have conducted several such experiments in Ralegan Siddhi and there are examples from many other villages in this book. In villages where people have planned for their land and water without any interference from the government, words such as hunger and unemployment have become alien. If we wish to construct a strong and self-sufficient country, we have to learn from these villages and change our system. We have to build a system where the power centres in villages and towns are gram sabhas and mohalla sabhas (community councils) respectively.

This book talks in detail about the meaning of change in the system. To achieve swaraj, or self-rule, what are the laws that we need to change and at what level? What will be the system of gram sabhas and Parliament in a true democracy? Every person who is dreaming of change needs to understand the answers to these questions. I believe this book is the manifesto of the India of tomorrow. I hope it will inspire people looking for answers to problems of unemployment, violence, corruption, inflation, Naxalism and untouchability.

August 2012   ANNA HAZARE

PREFACE

The year 2011 will be known as the year of the anti-corruption movement or the Anna agitation. In the past few years many corruption scams have come to the fore in our country—for example, the Rs 76,000-crore 2G scam, the Rs 70,000-crore Commonwealth Games scam and the Rs 20,000-crore Karnataka Wakf Board scam. The list is endless. All these scams and the ever-increasing inflation have left the people totally shaken.

In 2011, when a fakir from Ralegan Siddhi, a village in Maharashtra, spoke out against corruption, the whole country took to the streets in support. Anna Hazare demanded that a Jan Lokpal Bill against corruption be implemented so that the corrupt could be punished, sent to jail and their property seized by the government to make up for the losses it had incurred. Our anti-corruption laws are so lacking in conviction that it is almost impossible to punish the corrupt. Such cases drag on for years in the courts and no one is ever punished. Anna wanted all of this to change. He asked for a strong Jan Lokpal Bill which could ensure that the corrupt could be punished easily.

Anna went on a hunger strike three times in 2011, first in April at Jantar Mantar, Delhi; second in August at

Ramlila Maidan, Delhi; and third in December at the Azad Maidan in Mumbai. People in thousands took to the streets and hundreds of thousands gave their support. In almost every city and village, people could be seen waving the tricolour and shouting slogans like 'Bharat mata ki jai' and 'Inquilaab zindabad'. The political establishment was terrified on seeing the mass support for the agitation. On 27 August 2011, the entire Parliament unanimously agreed to the three demands put forth by Anna. But unfortunately, when the Parliament met in December 2011 and May 2012, they went back on their promise. Almost all the political parties in the Parliament double-crossed the nation.

The entire country wanted the Jan Lokpal Bill that Anna was championing. Surveys were carried out and people were asked which bill they wanted to be made into a law—the Lokpal Bill prepared by the government or the Jan Lokpal Bill made by the people. Over 90 per cent of the people said that they wanted the Jan Lokpal Bill. Many TV channels also conducted surveys that showed that 80 per cent people were in favour of the Jan Lokpal Bill. Despite such widespread support, the Parliament refused to pass it. Many politicians openly made fun of the people's movement during discussions in the Parliament.

It is then that questions were raised asking if laws should be made according to the wishes of the politicians only or should the people also be active participants? Is India really a democracy where only leaders have a say and people don't have a voice? Is it a democracy when the vote is cast only once every five years? And why is it that immediately after the vote is cast, people lose all rights to have a say in any matter? People are then forced to beg and plead in front of the leaders that they have elected. We thought a lot as to why it was that the government was not enacting a strong Lokpal Bill. Earlier, we used to think that if lakhs of people came out on the streets the government would have to listen to the collective voice due to fear that they might lose in the elections. In August 2011, lakhs of people took to the streets. In February 2012, the UPA actually lost a series of assembly elections. Still they did not pass a strong Lokpal Bill. We were surprised. In retrospect, it started becoming clear that if they passed a strong Lokpal Bill, some members of the Central cabinet, several chief ministers and chairpersons of several political parties would be in jail.

It became clear that these corrupt politicians were a direct obstacle to the Lokpal Bill. So it was demanded that a Special Investigation Team (SIT) headed by any three retired and honest Supreme Court judges should be set up to investigate these politicians. When the government did not listen, three of us, along with Annaji, sat on an indefinite fast from 25 July 2012 at Jantar

Mantar. By the tenth day of the fast it became clear that the government was in no mood to set up an SIT.

Twenty-three very eminent personalities, including Justice V.R. Krishna Iyer, Admiral (Retd) R.H. Tahiliani and Anupam Kher, among others, made an appeal to Annaji to give up the fast and provide a political alternative to the country. They wrote that the political establishment had become corrupt and that there was no hope from them. There was an urgent need to provide a political alternative. The question was put before the public. Many TV channels started conducting surveys. More than 90 per cent people said that Anna should provide a political alternative. Anna acceded to the public demand.

It is said that India did not gain independence in 1947; that was only a formal signing. The whites went and the natives took control of power. Earlier, the whites made life difficult and now the natives were doing so. During the British rule, India was governed from London. After 1947, India is being governed from Delhi and other state capitals. Our fight for independence was not only for liberation from the British. It was also for swaraj; for self-rule. There was a dream—that in independent India, the people will rule. There will be peace and happiness and justice will prevail. But that did not happen. The British went away but their system has remained in place. Corruption and injustice have increased with time. The rich have become richer and the poor have become poorer. There is no sight of swaraj, which was the reason for our fight for independence.

We want swaraj. Leaders and officers sitting in Delhi 'formulate' many illogical schemes on the pretext of development. Crores are spent on these schemes. The money reaches the pockets of the corrupt instead of the common man. We do not want this kind of development. If there is swaraj, there will be development for the people automatically. Swaraj means self-rule; our rule. We will be able to take decisions concerning our village, our town and our community. The laws made in the Parliament and the legislative assemblies will also be made with our consent and participation.

The democracy that exists in India today will have to change. Democracy should mean that for the five years after the vote is cast, the government functions according to the wishes of the people, and the views of the people are taken into account before making decisions. Is this possible? Can the government ask for the approval of 120 crore people before taking a decision?

It definitely can. There are many such governmental decisions in which people can participate directly. How can the people be active participants in any official programme? We have travelled to many parts of the country in search of answers to these questions and studied democracy in other countries and read history to learn from there. This book is a result of all these efforts.

In the absence of an appropriate law, some people have tried to implement swaraj in their respective villages. These people have been our inspiration. Anna Hazare changed the face of Ralegan Siddhi by implementing swaraj there. Similarly, Popatrao Pawar changed the face of Hivre Bazaar by bringing in direct partnership. Ilango completely changed the Kuthambakkam village of Chennai. There is a tribal village in Maharashtra, Menda Lekha, where villagers stood up against the forest department and other government offices. They transformed their village completely by insisting on taking all decisions in a general meeting of the entire gram sabha. Thakurdas Bang has written a lot on this issue. His books have been an inspiration to us and we have included a lot of his views in this book.

Does India today genuinely have democracy? Do the people have any say in government decisions? Why is our country's politics so tainted? This book tries to find answers to these questions. If we want to bring true democracy in India, then people must have direct participation in the working of the government. Governmental decisions must be taken with the approval of the people. This book presents a model for doing so.

Many people have helped in the writing of this book. I am deeply grateful to B.D. Sharma, B.C. Behar, Somu, Kapil Bajaj and Santosh Koli. Three councillors—Annapurna Mishra, Santosh Kumar and Harishankar

Kashyap—have played an important role in experimenting with mohalla sabhas in Delhi and we learnt a lot from them. I am grateful to the three of them. Last but not the least, Manish Sisodia and Swati Maliwal have been co-travellers on this journey, one that would not have been possible without them. To help the publisher sell the book to the maximum number of people at an affordable price, I am forgoing the royalty on the book.

August 2012   ARVIND KEJRIWAL

INTRODUCTION:
WHY THIS BOOK?

I used to work for the income tax department. Towards the end of the 1990s, the income tax department conducted a survey of several multinational companies. In the survey, many of these companies were caught red-handed evading taxes. They accepted their crimes and, without any appeal, they paid the entire amount. Had these companies been in any other country, their senior executives would have been sent to prison. The head of one such company on whom the raid had been conducted, a foreigner, threatened the income tax team. 'India is a very poor country. We have come to your country to help you. If you trouble us like this we will go away. You have no idea how powerful we are. If we want, we can get any law passed by your Parliament. We can even get you guys transferred.' A few days after this incident, a very senior member of our team was transferred out.

I did not pay much heed to the foreign gentleman's words at that point of time. I thought he must be troubled by the income tax department survey and was therefore talking like that. But the events of the past few years have made me believe the truth of his words. I now question myself, 'Do foreign powers actually control our Parliament?'

Let me cite an example. In 2008, the UPA government

3

had to prove its majority on the floor of the House. There were rumours that there was horsetrading of MPs. Some television channels showed certain members openly indulging in horsetrading. Those pictures shook the nation to its core. If MPs were being sold in this manner, what was the value of our vote? Tomorrow, they could be bought by America or Pakistan, or any other country. Who knows? This may already be happening. I shivered at this thought: 'Are we the citizens of a free nation? Does the Parliament of our country enact laws for the betterment of the people?'

When I read about the Civil Liability for Nuclear Damage Bill in the newspapers, all my fears seemed to be coming true. This bill states that if a foreign company were to set up a nuclear plant in India and if there was to be any accident, the company would be responsible for compensation to the tune of only Rs 1,500 crore. The world over, whenever there has been a nuclear accident, thousands have lost their lives and the losses have been in thousands of crores.

The Bhopal gas tragedy victims have so far received Rs 220 crore, which is considered fairly inadequate. In this context, Rs 1,500 crore does not seem much. How many Bhopal tragedies would a nuclear disaster equal? This bill further states that no criminal charges can be brought against the company and no case can be lodged against it. The company will be let off for a mere Rs 1,500 crore.

This bill gives me the impression that the lives of our people are being sold off for pennies. It is apparent that this bill openly favours foreign companies, putting on line the lives of the people of this nation. Why is our Parliament doing this? Either there is some kind of a pressure on our MPs, or some of our MPs have sold out to foreign companies.

After the court ruling on the Bhopal gas tragedy, newspapers were replete with stories of how politicians and senior leaders of our country helped the killers of the people of Bhopal run away from India, and also how they were accorded respect and accolades.

These events give rise to many questions in my mind: Is India in safe hands? Can we envision safe lives and futures in the hands of some of these politicians and bureaucrats?

It is not only foreign companies or foreign governments that exert influence on our government. Some politicians and bureaucrats can go to any lengths for money. Some ministers and officers have become puppets in the hands of powerful industrial houses. Recently, an exposé of a phone-tapping incident revealed that it was not the prime minister who decided portfolios for certain ministries but some of these industrial houses. It would not be an exaggeration to say that certain state governments and certain ministries in the Central government are being run by these industrial houses.

Some time back there was a newspaper report that a top industrialist planned to set up a private university in

Maharashtra. He met a Maharashtra minister who, in order to fulfil the industrialist's wish, agreed to present the Private University Bill in the vidhan sabha. Our vidhan sabhas are forever ready to enact laws to fulfil the wishes of industrial houses.

Our mines are being disposed of for a pittance to these industrial houses. For example, companies that acquire iron ore mines pay the government a royalty of a mere Rs 27 per ton. These companies then sell this same iron ore in the market at the rate of Rs 6,000 per ton (the cost of mining and cleaning the ore is about Rs 300 per ton). Isn't this a way of directly looting the country's resources?

In the same way, forests and rivers are being sold for peanuts; people's lands are being taken away and given to companies at a pittance. The natural resources and the riches of our country are in danger in the hands of these parties, politicians and bureaucrats. If we do not do something soon, they will sell off everything.

In view of all this, the Indian republic and Indian politics seem to be in jeopardy. It does not matter which leader or which party we vote for. They all seem to be the same.

We have tried out every party and every politician in the last sixty years. But there has been no improvement. One thing is very clear: it is pointless to change parties or leaders. We have to do something.

We have been working on various issues through our organization, 'Parivartan' (change), for the past ten years.

We have worked on the issues of ration and on the privatization of water, corruption in developmental works, etc. There were moments of success also. But we soon realized that success was momentary and illusionary. Till we were working on an issue, there seemed to be change in that area but as we moved on, that problem would only worsen. We began to feel helpless about how and what we could work on. Slowly, we realized that the root of all these problems lay in politics—because many politicians are in cahoots with the corrupt and criminal elements. The people have no say whatsoever. We can take the issue of rations, for example. If someone is stealing ration meant for the poor, we could complain to the food official, or the food minister. But they are part of the stealing. A part of the profits makes its way to them as well. So, can we expect justice by complaining to them? If the media creates pressure at any time, a few ration shops are shut down to placate people. But when the pressure is off, bribes are extended to ensure that those shops are in business again.

In this whole rigmarole the people have no power. They can only complain to the thieves to 'please take action against yourself' . . . and that is useless.

Therefore, it is obvious that the people should have the power to punish the corrupt instead of just being allowed to complain. It is imperative that the people have direct control over the entity through which decisions are to be taken by the people, and that bureaucrats and politicians should follow these decisions.

Is this possible? Is it possible to allow 120 crore people to take decisions regarding the law?

In theory, people are supreme in a democracy. It is the people who have given the Parliament and government the power to take decisions on their behalf. However, some of our MPs and MLAs have misused this power tremendously. They have shamelessly sold the people and their well-being for personal gain. Is it now time for us to withdraw from them the right to decide on our behalf? Is this possible? Won't this lead to anarchy?

We travelled widely, spoke to many people and researched extensively while seeking answers to these questions. Whatever we understood, we are presenting in this book. If, after reading it, you have certain doubts, do not hesitate to contact us. If you are in agreement with all that we have to say, join our movement in flesh, blood and spirit. There is no time to waste. The country's sovereignty and the country's resources are fast passing into the hands of foreign companies and governments. If we do not act soon, it will be too late.

THE PEOPLE HAVE NO SAY

The root cause of the problem is that in the political system of our country we cast our votes once in five years and for the next five we grovel in front of the same people we voted for and chose as our representatives. The people have no say whatsoever in the entire system.

NO CONTROL OVER GOVERNMENT EMPLOYEES

Suppose there is a situation in which the teacher in your village is not teaching properly, does not come on time or does not come at all. Can you do anything about this? No, we are helpless in this regard. We complain and no action is taken. Suppose the doctor in your local government hospital doesn't report on time, does not mete out proper treatment or fails to prescribe proper medicine, what can we do about it? Even if you complain, nobody will act on it.

The fair-price shopkeeper openly sells subsidized ration in the black market. But you cannot stop it anyway. You complain and nothing happens.

Similarly, you go to the police station to lodge a report, and they either don't enter it into a register or lodge a false complaint against you. You cannot do a thing.

So, if we look at it this way, it is evidently clear that we have no control over the government staff.

We pay taxes; even the poorest of the poor in this country pay tax. So much so, even a beggar pays tax—in the sense that when he buys soap from the market, he pays sales tax, excise duty and god knows how many other types of taxes. All these taxes are our money.

It is said that 70 per cent of the population survives on less than Rs 20 a day. So, if there are five people in a family, the monthly expenditure of this family is Rs 3,000. If we were to add all types of taxes levied, buying anything in the market would mean an average tax of 10 per cent. By this calculation, a poor family pays Rs 300 per month and Rs 3,600 per year in taxes. If there are a thousand families in a village, together they pay an average of Rs 36 lakh per year to the government. Over a period of ten years, therefore, the village would have paid about Rs 3.5 crore to the government in taxes.

This amount collected by the government in taxes is our money. And these government employees, officers and leaders are our servants. Their salary comes from our money. Our money runs their houses. Our money runs their air conditioners. All their cars with the red beacons, their petrol, and their servants come from our money.

And they treat us with contempt. Those whose salary

comes from our money, don't listen to us. We c
control our own servants. We cannot do anything aga
government doctors, teachers, fair-price shopkeepers,
policemen. Have you ever been to the office of a collecto.
Have you ever tried to meet him? He is never available
He is our servant and yet lords over us. His peon lords
over us. We simply have no control over all these
government employees whose salary comes from our
money.

NO CONTROL OVER GOVERNMENT MONEY

We have no control over government funds. How should
all this government money be spent? Where should it be
used? What are our needs? Nobody asks us. In Delhi, in
the name of the Commonwealth Games, the government
blew up Rs 70,000 crore. Perfectly-fine roads were
demolished and redone. Perfectly-fine footpaths were
broken up and redone. One newspaper reported that the
government was remaking footpaths for Rs 400 crore.

At the same time, MCD sweepers did not receive their
salaries for three months. Contractors have not been paid
for over five years. Yet, a helipad is being constructed
over the MCD building so that the helicopters of
politicians can land there.

When we approach the government with a problem, it
tells us that there are no funds. Take the example of

an't
nst
or
?

slum area in Delhi. People there don't
water. There is no secondary school and no
. Whenever the government is approached,
is no money. But the government installed
worth Rs 60 lakh in the same locality a few
go! People don't have potable water and the
ment installed water fountains! Can there be
hing more hilarious than this? These fountains have
worked for even a single day, and how could they?
here is no water in the area.

It is obvious that the government does have money but it is being used on things that are unnecessary.

Take an example of villages. Villages have various problems but the money that reaches them is given to them under strange schemes. People sit in Delhi and state capitals and decide what the issues plaguing 120 crore people of the country are, what our needs are and how money should be spent in a particular area. Various schemes such as old-age pension, widow pension, NREGA, ration, etc., are formulated by leaders and officials sitting in Delhi, Lucknow, Bhopal and other capital cities.

We went to Khajoori village of West Bengal. The sarpanch there told us that the village had received Rs 6 crore. But they were unable to spend Rs 20 lakh out of that to build a school for the village because the money was in a 'tied' fund. The entire amount of money was tied to various schemes. Some of it was to be given out as old-age pension, some of it would be used for building houses under the Indira Awaas scheme, some of it was kept aside for widows' pension, some of it was for this and some of it was for that.

But our needs are different. We could, for example, be interested in irrigating our land. Or we may want some doctors in our village. Unfortunately, it is decided beforehand in Delhi how much money is going to be spent under what head.

We went to a village in Orissa. Sixty-three families were suffering from cholera in that village. The nearest hospital was 25 kilometres away and there was no transport to get there. The village panchayat had more than Rs 6 lakh but the entire amount was in 'tied' funds. It had come from some scheme. They could not hire any vehicle with that money to take the sick to the hospital. As a result, seven persons died. So what good was that money? What good is money that we cannot use to save lives?

Take another example. Some officer in Delhi must have had a dream. He dreamt that if every village started collecting/harvesting its water, the country would not have the problem of water scarcity. So a writ was issued. A scheme was formulated at the very top. The scheme was called 'Our village, Our water'. Any village that would construct civil structures to harvest its own water would be given upto Rs 1 lakh. The scheme started in Delhi and reached a state capital. It reached every collector of each zilla in the state. A zilla collector called all the sarpanches of a particular zilla and told them about the scheme and asked them to implement it in their villages. The sarpanch of a village went back and collected all the village folks and told them about the scheme. Everyone started laughing upon hearing about it because the village faces floods every year and they do not want to retain their water but send it out!

Such are the senseless schemes that come from Delhi. The problems in the entire country cannot be solved by schemes. I strongly believe that no problem can be solved by schemes formulated in Delhi. The situation of two neighbouring villages is so different that it cannot be understood by someone sitting in Delhi. It is impossible to think of a solution in this way.

BPL (BELOW POVERTY LINE) POLITICS

All these government schemes have turned people into beggars. Many of these schemes are formulated under the aegis of eradication of poverty, in the name of the poor, and fall under the BPL scheme. We have to understand BPL politics.

These BPL schemes are hatched to garner more votes. They say that they are a government of the poor and are making schemes for them, but they know from the word go that this money is never going to reach the poor.

We met a senior politician of our country. We said to him, 'Stop making these schemes in Delhi and just send the money to the villages. Let the people of every village decide what they want to do with the money.' He replied, 'Do you have any idea how many alligators are there around each scheme? If we were to stop coming up with these schemes, our government would soon be out of power. All the parties would withdraw support.' It therefore means that they know that the money is not reaching the poor and it never will. Then why are they persisting with these schemes? On one hand, politicians try and show that they are a government for the poor by formulating these schemes and on the other hand, they also know quite well that this money is going to go into their pockets. These schemes are there only so that they can lure voters and fill their own coffers.

These schemes have also had a very bad effect on the people. You can go to any village. People there will walk up to you and demand to know why their name is not on the BPL list. They ask for their name to be included in the BPL list. What is the meaning of BPL? It implies a person who is helpless, who has no money, and who is totally incapable and wants society to help him. Look at the absurdity of the situation. Everybody wants to be a beggar. Everybody wants to be on a list of beggars. There is a race to become beggars. How is such a country ever going to progress?

I have travelled a lot in the country but I never met a man who told me that he had once been on the BPL list, was a declared beggar but is now self-dependent and wants to be out of the BPL list. Nobody wishes to be self-dependent. These schemes seem to be destroying people's mindsets.

Therefore, what we have understood is that first, there is no control over the government employees, and second, there is no control over the use of government funding.

NO CONTROL OVER GOVERNMENT POLICIES AND LAWS

Our government enacts many laws and policies. We have neither control nor any say in these. In the introduction to this book, there was a mention of how our Parliament is passing some laws under the influence of foreign companies and foreign governments. In doing so, it is putting the lives of the people of this country on the line for a few pennies.

We vote. We choose governments and the government does not ask what kind of laws we want. Before any law is enacted, those who are consulted are foreign companies and foreign governments.

Therefore, the third problem is that the common people do not have any kind of control over the Parliament or vidhan sabhas.

NO CONTROL OVER NATURAL RESOURCES

We have no control over the natural resources of our country. Natural resources, such as water, forests, land and minerals, are being taken away from us and being given to companies.

Land

The entire country is on fire on the question of land acquisition. Almost every state has at least three or four places where a mass movement is on against land acquisition. Land is being acquired against the will of the people. People have the following basic objections to land acquisition:

(a) Many farmers say that they will not give their land. They fail to understand how the schemes for which land is being acquired will benefit them. The government has failed to convince the people. In most places, land is being acquired for distribution to various companies. It is beyond the comprehension of people how a government chosen by them can acquire land for the benefit of a few companies in the face of stiff opposition by the people.

(b) Some want a better price for their land. The rates at which land is being taken away from farmers are very low. In practically every agitation people are fighting over the price of the land. Land is taken away and rates decided without consultation with the people. Worse, this money doesn't reach the people for years.

(c) In many tribal areas where land has been acquired, if the farmer has received a lakh or so of compensation, it is not going to sustain him for long. What will they do with this paltry sum? All such farmers are left to die of hunger when their land is taken away.

(d) Very often, when entire villages are acquired, landowners get compensation but those who work as labourers on that land, those who run shops or are otherwise engaged, get nothing. All of them are rendered unemployed.

(e) Therefore, land acquisition under various schemes nets the companies a good profit, and some officers and politicians get a good bribe, while the farmers are rendered unemployed and the landless hungry. The governments need to explain to the people how this is in the common man's interest.

We have to understand the land acquisition scenario well. For example, if a company wishes to set up a plant in a village, it does not come to the village directly. The company approaches the state government. Now, a corrupt official or politician in the state government pockets a good amount of money and grants permission to 'set up a factory in the village'. And then, making use of the state machinery's clout and the police force, people are ousted from their land, which is taken away for a paltry sum and given to the companies.

God alone knows how many people have lost their land under the Special Economic Zone (SEZ) scheme. Do you know that some years ago, in a single meeting of the Central government, upto thirty SEZ projects used to be passed? These SEZ projects are huge. How can you approve them in a meeting that lasts two minutes? The approval is, therefore, just a formality. There were rumours that money was being made in return for approval. A company that pays a bribe is likely to get its project approved in no time. The projects of companies that do not pay bribes are rejected.

Thus, people have no control over even their own land.

Minerals

In many cases, the mineral ore mines of our country are either being leased or sold to companies at a very low price. There is an abundance of minerals in our country, especially coal, iron and bauxite. These were not created in a day but through a natural process that took thousands of years. But our government is selling them to private companies at unwarrantedly low prices. Private companies do not use these resources for the betterment of the country. They mine these resources and sell them in international markets for huge profits.

The rate at which minerals are being mined, very soon we won't have any left. In some parts of the country minerals are being depleted at a very fast rate. For example, Goa used to export a large quantity of iron to Japan a few years ago but it is being said that good iron is no longer available in Goa. The iron from Bailadila mines in Karnataka is considered the best in the world. In the fast few years this iron has been mined so extensively that it is estimated that the Bailadila mines will be empty in about twenty-five years. Interestingly, China has iron ore mines but there is no mining there at present. China will probably start mining once the rest of the world has no ores left.

It is obvious that the mineral resources of the country are not safe in the hands of some of these officials and politicians. Such politicians will one day sell off the entire country.

Second, when private companies are granted permits for these mines, people living in these areas are ousted. The governments of Orissa, Jharkhand and Chhattisgarh have signed various deals with different companies for mining, under which many acres of land is being taken away from the tribal people and given to these companies. Many areas in these states have turned into a battlefield between the people and the police. This is also responsible for the increase in Naxal activities in these areas. Tribal land is sold off to companies for paltry sums. The companies earn huge profits from mining there and the tribals face unemployment and hunger. Their villages and society are ruined.

Third, these companies do not take precautions while mining. They pollute the environment and the price has to be paid by the people living nearby. When people complain, the government official dismisses all complaints as he would have had pocketed a bribe by that time.

For instance, there is a village near Ranchi that has ONGC oil wells. Once, some of the wells started emitting methane gas, something that had happened earlier in nearby villages as well. When there is a leakage of methane gas, you cannot light any fire as the whole area will go up in flames. People were very worried. But they had no option. They could not do anything against ONGC. They complained to the collector but he said that action was being taken. He was so casual in his approach that it seemed as if nothing had happened. He said that methane leaks were a common occurrence in the area. People had to accept what he said and live with the danger. The gas leak did not bother the collector because it did not affect his life at all.

Thus, people have no control whatsoever over the nation's resources, their pillage or the pollution caused by the mining of these resources.

Forests

Bir Singh Markam is a tribal from a village in Bastar district of Chhattisgarh. He grows corn on a small piece of land in the forest. His entire family used to survive on this. In 1998, the forest department arrested Bir Singh and seventy-five other people from his village. They were charged with unlawful occupation of forest land and thrown into jail.

After he was released, Markam had to go to the courts at least twenty times. The court is nearly 30 kilometres away from his village. Every visit to the court took a toll on his spirit. In the end, to repay all his debts and pay fines, he had to sell his bulls.

There are hundreds of thousands of tribals like Markam who have got a raw deal after independence. Till 1947, when the British tried to capture tribal land, they were dealt a strong blow. The British then adopted a policy of not integrating the tribal area under their direct control. Rules and laws applicable to the entire country were not applicable to the tribal areas. These areas were called the 'excluded areas', which meant that they were outside the purview of British power.

The Indian Constitution was framed in 1950 and Indian laws were applicable to all tribal areas. The tribals had no papers to show the ownership of the land on which they had been living for centuries. Outsiders took advantage of this and usurped the land. Similarly, tribals whose livelihood was dependent on the forests (some of them even lived in the forest) became criminals on their own land in their own forests because these had been declared government property.

Forest officials, and even employees at a lower level in the forest department, started harassing the tribals in their villages. Although these tribals had been living in the forest for centuries, they had no papers to prove it. Therefore, they were considered squatters. Officials would stop them from farming on the land, cutting wood, picking fruits and leaves or grazing their flock. Elephants were brought in to raze the farms. Officials would ruin the soil by sprinkling acacia seeds. People were beaten up and their crops destroyed. The forest officials were in a way doing their job—safeguarding the forests.

On one hand, the tribals were being forced out of the forests and, on the other, some of the forest officials, contractors and politicians together were looting the forests. Forests that were safe under the patronage of the tribals for centuries started disappearing under the control of the forest department. A few examples are:

(a) Every year the government awards contracts for tendu (*Diospyros melonoxylon*) leaves. Every contractor gets a contract for 1,500 to 2,000 bags/sacks. The contract is for this amount but what he takes out after bribing the forest official is anybody's guess. The smallest contractor reportedly makes more than Rs 15 lakh in a year. But they pay the tribals less than 30 paisa per bundle to get the leaves, an amount which, under Naxal pressure, has been hiked to Re 1 per bundle.

(b) The government allows the paper mills to harvest tons of bamboo at a very low price for years on end. These mill owners pay the tribals 10 to 20 paisa per bundle to harvest the bamboo on which they earn huge profits.

Water

In many cities of our country, water is being distributed through foreign companies. The Delhi government too was about to sell the water management of Delhi to some foreign companies. But the people's movement put an end to that.

Even the rivers of our country are being sold. In Chhattisgarh, the entire Shivnath river was entrusted to a company. Now if anybody needs to use the water from the river, be it for irrigation, drinking, or washing clothes, it cannot be done without permission from the company.

Almost every river has a dam on it. So many dams are being constructed on the Ganga that the river might well lose its identity after some time. It will end up being just a stream of water flowing between dams. We agree that the country needs electricity. But can we deny the fact that the country also needs rivers? Many countries have laws to allow the national rivers to flow in their original state. But there are no such laws in our country. In the past few years, judging from the speed at which private companies have been awarded contracts to build dams, it seems that some of our officials and leaders are more interested in the bribe that is extended rather than the electricity that is to be generated. At this rate all our rivers will turn into dirty drains in a few years.

All these examples make one thing definitely clear: that our natural resources are endangered in the hands of corrupt politicians and officials. If we do not act soon, they will sell our entire country off.

IS THIS DEMOCRACY?

It is now obvious that we have no control over this entire system. We cannot do anything against government employees. We have no say in government policies. There is no participation in lawmaking, little control over the Parliament or the vidhan sabhas. Our natural resources such as water, forest and land are being thoughtlessly sold off. We have no control over that either.

Is this democracy? Is democracy all about casting your vote once in five years and then letting these parties and their leaders rule the roost?

This cannot be a democracy. There is something wrong somewhere. The basic problem in our country is that there is no democracy.

We want democracy. The politics of voting once in five years is no longer acceptable. The people want a direct participation in power. The people shall take decisions, and politicians and officials will have to implement them.

When we say such things people often ask: How can the people take decisions? People will end up fighting amongst themselves.

But in this country people have been taking decisions for centuries now. It is indeed unfortunate that we have forgotten our own culture. Where did India learn democracy? Many people believe that we did so from America. Some say we learnt it from the British. The truth is that India has had democracy since the time of Buddha. In fact, it was much stronger then. Vaishali was the first democracy in the world. In those days there were no elections and the king's son would be king, but he had no powers. All decisions were taken in the village's gram sabha. The king had to accept whatever the people of the village and gram sabha said. Today, we elect a king every five years but he doesn't listen to us. Those days the king wasn't elected but he did as the people dictated.

The following story is from those times. There was once a king in Vaishali. It was a day in court; the king as well as other people were in attendance. Some people pointed to a girl and asked her to become a courtesan. The girl said, 'That's fine with me. I can become a

31

courtesan but I have a condition. I want the king's castle. If you give me the castle I am willing to become a courtesan.' The issue was placed before the gram sabha and passed. The king was sitting there and listening to everything. He got flustered and said, 'How is this possible? The castle is mine. How can you give my castle to this girl?' The people then said, 'This castle is not yours. We have given it to you. We pay taxes. It is made with our money. Today the people of this country are taking this castle from you and giving to this girl. If you want a castle, make another one.' The king had to vacate the castle and give it to the girl; he made another one for himself. To ask somebody to become a courtesan or to make somebody a courtesan is a wrong custom but we can learn one thing from this story: the people and the politics of that period were very powerful.

The president of our country lives in a huge house. The Rashtrapati Bhawan is a 340-acre house in the heart of Delhi. In the same city, 40 per cent people live in slums like insects. They don't have enough place to sleep. There are ten people in one hut. If we were to pass a resolution that the president of our country should live in a smaller house, do you think he/she will accept it? Never.

In New Delhi, all bureaucrats and ministers have big bungalows. Some of these huge houses are occupied by just a husband and wife. If we were to tell our officers and politicians to vacate their houses and live in smaller ones so that more people in Delhi could have homes, would they agree? Never.

There was democracy when people passed resolutions and kings vacated their castles. There is no democracy today when we can pass a resolution but are not able to construct a road in front of our house, we can't check on schoolteachers, or ensure proper service from doctors.

It was in times gone by that people made decisions and the king implemented them. The scenario in which village people had complete and direct control over organizational matters went on till 1860. What the irrigation management would be, or how schools would be run would be decided by the people themselves. Many people invaded our country but they only took control of the Central government. They did not touch the village system. They only increased or decreased taxes while in power at the Centre.

In 1830, the then acting governor-general, Lord Metcalfe, wrote that the foundation of this country was the gram sabhas. People would meet and the whole village would take joint decisions. And that is how the villages functioned. In 1860, the British enacted a law to break these sabhas. They had understood that if these sabhas were not broken the British could not establish a stronghold in this country. They brought a law and established the collector's rule. All the powers that were earlier with the people and the gram sabhas were taken away and given to a British collector. Earlier, the people of the village managed the irrigation system; now an irrigation department was set up. Earlier, people managed the system of education in the villages; now an education department was created. For every system there was now a department and a British officer called the 'collector' was made the in-charge of everything.

Unfortunately, in 1947, at the time of independence, we could not return the power of the people to the people; we could not return the decision-making powers to the gram sabhas. We removed a British collector and in his place installed an Indian one. We let the rest of the British system intact. Till those rights and powers are not given back to the people, there is no scope for change. There will be no freedom till then.

THE SHORTCOMINGS OF THE CURRENT PANCHAYATI RAJ

Many people ask what is new in what we are demanding. Even today we have the panchayats. It is good that there is direct participation of the people through the panchayati raj. That was the system before the British came to our country. But after independence, the system that came into force in the name of panchayati raj has only ended up providing opportunities to officials and politicians to make money rather than empowering the people.

Unfortunately, the panchayat has ended up as a mere agency for implementing the schemes proposed by the Central and state governments rather than facilitating self-administration. Most of the schemes are formulated in Delhi or the state capitals. The panchayats are only authorized to implement them. Gram sabhas, that is the entire village community sitting together for dialogue, are very rare. This is because nobody is interested. Even if a meeting is convened, very few people turn up because they know that their demands in the sabha will not be met.

There are many shortcomings in our panchayati raj system but the following problems are strangling it completely:

(a) The panchayats have very limited powers. They have no power over government officials and no say in the disbursement of official funds.

(b) The very few powers that have been allocated to the panchayat are vested in the sarpanch or the pradhan. In any panchayat the buck stops with the pradhan. He takes all the decisions. The gram sabhas, that is to say, the people, have been given no power under most of the panchayati raj laws. The gram sabha can only advice the sarpanch; whether he pays heed to their advice is up to him.

(c) That is why many of the sarpanches have become corrupt. The people have no power to take any action against a corrupt sarpanch. They can only watch helplessly.

(d) The collector has the right to act against a corrupt, useless and irresponsible sarpanch at any point. He can suspend him. And that is why the sarpanches are always scared of the collector and the block development officer. Just as the governor is the representative of the Central government in the states, the collector works as a representative of the state government in any district. Fortunately, the governor does not have many rights and cannot interfere in the working of the state government. Unfortunately, however, the collector has unlimited rights of interference in the working of the panchayat. The state governments are interfering in the daily functions of the panchayats in an unjust manner through the collectors. Let us take a look at some examples of the shortcomings of the current panchayati system.

TREE PLANTATION DRIVE IN BHONDSI VILLAGE

Every village requires water and soil and crops and irrigation. But the irrigation department is not bothered about the soil. The soil department is not bothered about the water. The water department is not bothered about the trees. The department dealing with trees is not bothered about anything else. Each department has its annual targets and that is all they want to achieve.

Bhondsi is a village in Haryana, near Delhi. The forest department once had a target of planting more trees in this village, as it did not have enough. To achieve this they showered acacia seeds all over the village from a helicopter. These particular seeds were sprayed because this tree grows very fast. They had to meet a target. They had to show that this area had a thick growth of trees. But acacia draws a lot of water from the soil, so the trees have completely destroyed the water system there. As a result, the water level went down alarmingly. The aim was to do good but all it did was cause harm.

This is what our panchayati raj is like. What trees should be planted in an area is neither decided by the people nor by the panchayats.

CITY GARBAGE IN KUTHAMBAKKAM

Kuthambakkam is a village near Chennai. For some time now a search has been on for a place to dump the garbage of six cities near Chennai. The government's evil eye suddenly fell on the flat grasslands of this village. This village has approximately 100 acres of grasslands on which about 5,000 animals graze. The collector there issued an order and acquired seventy acres of land so that the garbage for those six towns could be dumped there. Obviously, the people of the village were enraged. First, what would their animals eat? Second, why would the garbage of six towns be dumped there? Weren't the people of this village human beings? Why would they have to live with so much garbage? What was shocking was that the collector had acquired the land without taking the people into confidence. People went to the court but lost because the collector is authorized to acquire land in this manner.

Is this panchayati raj, where neither the panchayat nor the sarpanch or the people have any power? In the prevailing panchayati raj system, the collector and the government rob the people of their land without the panchayat having any say in the matter. They dump garbage from neighbouring towns in our villages.

THE FARCE OF NREGA

Money today moves from top to bottom. But it never reaches the bottom. Every officer is determined to spend all of it at his/her level. For example, according to the National Rural Employment Guarantee Act (NREGA), 4 per cent of the money is for contingency. This means that this percentage should be used for providing facilities to those who work on NREGA projects, such as creating a crèche for children of women working on the projects, arranging clean drinking water for labourers, etc.

But, in many districts, the collectors do whatever they feel like. They do not let the money trickle down to the villages. In one village in Uttar Pradesh, the district magistrate himself kept the 4 per cent contingency fund of the NREGA. He bought new cupboards and rugs and distributed them in the villages. The people did not need those rugs and cupboards. Lawfully, the gram sabha should have a say in the way this money is spent. But because money travels from top to bottom, officials in the middle spend the money wilfully. The people have no say in the matter and have no control over the officials, and so they cannot do anything about this high-handedness.

THE PANCHAYATS CANNOT EVEN BUY BROOMS

The law says that if a sarpanch is not working well, does not attend meetings and is corrupt, the collector has the authority to take action against him. He can constitute an enquiry and remove him from his post. There are 2,000 villages under the purview of the collector. How will he know whether any sarpanch is doing his job well or not? Who would know better—the people of the village or the collector? But the authority to take action against the sarpanch is vested in the collector and not in the people. So what has happened is that the collectors who are corrupt have started demanding protection money (*hafta*) from the sarpanches. Those who pay are safe and those who do not, have false cases against them. Sarpanches are thus forced into unlawful activities through threats of false cases being registered against them.

Let us understand through an example how the panchayati raj system is resulting in the misuse of the sarpanch. The state governments have total authority over the sarpanch or the pradhan and they in turn can be easily pressurized into doing unlawful things for this very reason.

In Uttar Pradesh, the state government told a contractor to provide cleaning supplies to all the villages of the state. Wheel barrows, bowls and all kinds of implements for cleaning drains were required. The contractor was told to give all this to the sarpanch. The contractor went and dumped all this in front of the sarpanch's house. The block development officer (BDO) called up the sarpanch, asking him to pay for all this. The sarpanch had no option but to pay, else the BDO would institute some enquiry or the other against him.

On paper, the panchayat had bought all the supplies but in reality the state government had illegally got a contractor to provide all the supplies. All the sarpanches are instructed on the phone that 'he will come with the supplies. Take them and make the payment'.

The same thing is happening in the Sarv Shiksha Abhiyan (SSA), the movement for education for all. The panchayats are authorized to buy supplies for the SSA. But here also one will come across examples of high-handedness. Every village gets money in its village education fund under the SSA. But in some districts of Uttar Pradesh, it has been found that a contractor is told at the district level to rectify the electricity problems in all the schools of all the villages. He goes to the village school but either does nothing or does a very bad job. He supplies substandard goods. Then the sarpanch of every village is asked on the phone to make the contractor's payment. This is how state governments and district officials are lording over sarpanches.

PANCHAYAT SECRETARY—OF THE PANCHAYAT OR THE STATE GOVERNMENT?

According to the law, the panchayat secretary or all officials of the village are to be appointed by the state government. The state government decides what the work of the secretary will be. Who do you think will make a better appointment for the panchayat secretary of the village—the villagers or the state government? Who should decide what his duties will be—the people or the government? What will the state government know about what each village requires?

THE STORY OF THE 'BACKWARD REGION GRANT FUND'

The Central government has a scheme called the 'Backward Region Grant Fund', under which it sanctions money for the most backward districts. The scheme clearly states that the gram sabhas will decide what the people require. The fund will be used on projects decided by the gram sabha.

There are about 250 districts in the country where this scheme is being implemented. In Haryana, there are two districts—Sirsa and Mahendragarh—where this scheme is on. When we visited these districts we found that no gram sabha meeting had been convened and the fund was being spent without the gram sabha's intervention. On making enquiries, it was learnt that the money was being credited in the collector's account. According to the law, the collector will disburse the money according to the programme prepared by the gram sabha. However, collectors are using the fund according to their own will instead of asking for proposals from the gram sabha.

For example, the collector decides that schools have to be constructed in these hundred villages. He then calls a contractor and tells him to build schools in these villages. The sarpanches of these villages are then asked to provide fake proposals that say that their gram sabhas want schools to be constructed in their villages.

Some senior politicians are also pressurizing the collectors to use the Backward Region Grant Fund according to their whims and fancies. In one particular village, it came to light that a politician had a large piece of farmland. He pressurized the collector to get a lot of digging done around his land. If the gram sabha was involved, such a decision would never have been taken.

In Sirsa district, some young boys from eighteen villages made a sincere effort and actually organized gram sabha meetings and sent proposals to higher authorities. This scheme clearly states that proposals will be formulated by gram sabhas and sent to the collector. The collector will approve these proposals and disburse the funds accordingly. In spite of this, the district collector in Sirsa had not approved the proposal sent by these eighteen villages even after a whole year.

CONCLUSION

There are thousands of such examples in the entire country to show that the panchayati raj in no way guarantees direct participation of the people in governance and politics. The power has to be taken from the state government, the collector and the sarpanch, and vested in the gram sabhas.

EXAMPLES FROM OTHER COUNTRIES

We also studied the democratic system in other countries. What happens in America? What is the situation in Brazil? How do things operate in Switzerland? We are presenting some of the more successful and better democratic structures for you.

AMERICA—WALMART LOST

In America, no decision is taken without the participation of the people, be it at the local, city, municipality, or even the county level. In many towns, regular weekly meetings are held. For example, there is a town called Middle Town. If you visit its website you will see that there is a public meeting every Monday at five in the evening. People are summoned to the town hall, and they take all the decisions in these meetings. The town is governed accordingly.

Walmart is an American company that wishes to start business in India. Many people feel that if it comes to India, unemployment will increase. The issue of unemployment is altogether a different one. What is more important is to see who decided whether it should come to our country or not. Only two people are authorized to take this decision in our country—the prime minister and the finance minister. We are not asked questions such as these at all. We are the ones who will lose jobs and face unemployment and poverty, yet we have no say.

The same company wanted to open a shop in a town in Oregon state. Every house in that town received a notice telling them that Walmart wanted to open a shop in their town and they were asked if it should be allowed to do so. They were all asked to come for a town hall meeting at a designated time on a particular date to take a decision on this. People gathered in the town hall and said, 'We don't want Walmart to open a shop here as that will result in smaller shops shutting down.' Walmart could not open a shop there. A company that could not open a shop in its own country wants to set up business in India and we are not even asked.

BRAZIL—A BUDGET THAT IS PREPARED ON THE STREETS

Take the example of Brazil. Porto Alegre is a small town in Brazil. About 30 to 40 per cent of the town's population lives in slums. The Workers' Party came to power in Porto Alegre in 1990. In those days there were no roads, drinking water, electricity, or sewer connections in the slum area. Many people were illiterate. The party decided that the budget for Porto Alegre would not be made in the municipal corporation's hall or in the council but on the city's streets. They divided Porto Alegre into small areas. Now people meet in their respective areas at the beginning of every year and put forward their requirements. Some say they have bad roads, some ask for water, some want the sewer repaired and some want teachers to be appointed. All the demands are put together and then the budget for the town is worked out. What is a budget? Why should it be made within closed halls and assemblies? Budgets should be formulated on the streets with the people. A budget is meant to figure out how best to spend government money for the people.

The result of this experiment was very good. The party has won elections consecutively for the past fifteen years. The World Bank report says that there has been tremendous development because of this experiment. Earlier, there was no potable water and now 98 per cent of the houses have access to drinking water. Around 87 per cent of the houses have sewer connections now. There is 100 per cent literacy. And the World Bank report also says that there has been a substantial decrease in corruption.

SWITZERLAND—A PARLIAMENT THAT RUNS ON THE PEOPLE'S WISHES

Take the example of Switzerland. It is recognized as the best democracy in the world. This is so because if 50,000 people in Switzerland sign a petition and ask for a law, it has to be presented as an act in the Parliament. And if 100,000 people sign a petition, it has to be presented as an amendment in the Parliament. In this way, people have direct control over the Constitution and the process of law making.

If 50,000 people were to sign a petition and send it to the Indian Parliament, I doubt if there would even be an acknowledgement of receipt of that letter.

We can see how there is direct participation of the people in governance in other countries. But in our country we are forever begging; we have no say in our own governance.

ALL HAIL THE PEOPLE

We cast our vote once every five years and hand over the right to make all our decisions to certain people. We hand over so much power that some of them become either corrupt—putting us and our lives at stake—or power drunk.

This has to be changed. We need to ensure that decisions are taken by the people and that officials and politicians only implement them. If they don't, we should be able to remove them. When we say this, people wonder: how can the common man take such decisions? How can a hundred crore people take decisions? They say it is not possible.

It is absolutely possible. There are gram sabhas in our villages. The Constitution decrees it. A gram sabha does not mean the panchayat. A panchayat is a few chosen people from the village—the sarpanch, the pradhan or the mukhiya, and a ward member. A gram sabha means a meeting of the *entire* village in the open.

CONTROL OVER GOVERNMENT OFFICIALS

The gram sabha should have the authority and right to decide about issues related to the village. There should be amendments in the panchayati raj and other laws so that if a teacher does not teach well or does not come to school on time, the gram sabha should have the authority to stop his/her salary.

If the government doctor is not treating his patients properly, the gram sabha in its meeting should be able to stop his salary. If the shopkeeper of subsidized rations is stealing from the people, the gram sabha should be able to close down his shop. If the police constable does not take the villager's complaints or tries to register false cases against him or her, the gram sabha should be able to stop his salary.

What is your opinion? Do you think things will improve if we do this? We feel that there will be many improvements. Everyone—the teacher, doctor, shopkeeper, or constable—will work better. The gram sabha should have direct control over state officials through the people.

Teachers in villages should be appointed by the gram sabha. At the moment, the state government appoints 10,000 teachers in one go and this involves bribery and corruption. What will a teacher appointed after a payment of bribes, teach the children?

The Right to Information Act has brought to light the fact that there is not a single teacher in many schools in Jharkhand. For example, in Vamni High School Kenuga, Saraikela, in Kharsawa, there are 310 students but not a single teacher. There is a single Bengali teacher in ten classes of 435 students in the school in Sirum. It is the responsibility of the state government to appoint teachers. People have written to the government many times but have received no reply. Will our children wait for the benevolence of the state government forever? Does this not amount to playing a cruel joke with their lives?

This system needs to be shut down. The people whose children are studying in these schools should have the authority to appoint teachers and to remove them when need be. Those who go to government hospitals for treatment should have the authority to appoint and remove doctors there. The power should be in the hands of the people. The responsibility of appointing all government officials at the village level, giving them orders, punishing them and, if need be, removing them, should be directly vested in the people through the gram sabha.

This will have many benefits. Today, state governments appoint city people to teach in the villages. They get paid Rs 15,000 per month. Even then they don't come to the villages to teach. Some of them even feel ashamed to sit with village folks.

If the village people were to appoint the teacher directly, it would provide employment to the educated of the village and they would even do so at a salary of just Rs 5,000 per month. And if they do not teach properly they could be punished as well.

The law should be changed in such a manner that the gram sabha has the power to issue orders to any official of the district or the block and summon him to its meetings. It should be able to tell the collector what to do. And if the collector does not comply, it should be able to summon him, the SDM, the tehsildar, the BDO and the ration officer. And if any of these officials do not heed the summons, the gram sabha should have the power to punish them.

The gram sabha should have the right to ask any official up to the state level for information related to their respective villages. There are strange schemes formulated with the villages in mind. Therefore, the gram sabha should have a right to know what kind of schemes are being prepared, or what decisions are being taken for them.

CONTROL OVER GOVERNMENT MONEY/FUNDS

Funds released by the state and the Central governments should be in the form of an untied fund (not tied to any scheme). We do not want any government scheme at all; we do not want old-age pension, widow pension, or NREGA, or Indira Awaas Yojna.

It is better to give a village Rs 3 crore in untied funds than Rs 5 crore in tied funds. Let the people of the village meet in a gram sabha and decide how much money will be spent on irrigation, how much on education and how much on health. Let the village decide the amount to be spent under whichever head.

Similarly, let the village people decide who falls in the BPL category. What will be the parameters for that? In Hong Kong, a person who doesn't have an air-conditioner is considered to be a BPL person. In Delhi, a rickshaw-puller earns more than Rs 5,000 per month but despite that he is unable to sustain himself and lives like an insect in the slums. But 5,000 rupees is a good amount for a family in the village.

It is wrong to decide the parameters for the entire country while sitting in Delhi. The parameters for being in the BPL category are very different in Delhi than in Kalahandi.

The villagers should sit together and decide whether a man who doesn't have a house will be given one. He will get a house from the gram sabha fund. People won't be dependent on the Indira Awaas Yojna, under which the government sanctions two houses for every village today. Owing to corruption, these are given to people who don't need them at all. Let the people of the village decide who is actually homeless. Let all such people be given houses. If there is somebody who is not earning and is unable to feed himself, let the village decide whether to support him with ration for some time so that he does not die of hunger. It should be the responsibility of the gram sabha to see that no one dies of hunger in their village. It should be their responsibility to ensure that everyone has a roof over their heads and everyone has clothes to wear. Let this be decided by the people and the gram sabhas. Let this money be spent in this way.

Take, for example, the fact that someone may want to start a business and someone may want to farm the land. When they need money, they end up in the clutches of moneylenders and their life becomes miserable. They have to pay an interest of up to 100 per cent. They could borrow money from the gram sabha and the gram sabha could lend it money if it received it in untied funds.

In many parts of the country, farmers are committing suicide. This could be stopped if gram sabhas had untied funds and were able to offer assistance to helpless farmers.

Third, many times after harvesting, the farmers don't have a place to store the crop. If it rains, the entire crop is ruined. If the gram sabha has untied funds at its disposal, the villagers, if they so wish, could construct a storehouse for the crop.

If the people of the village wanted to set up a factory they could use that money. Kuthambakkam is a village near Chennai whose sarpanch, Ilango, has done some amazing work. He used to be a chemical engineer who quit his job fifteen years ago and became the sarpanch of Kuthambakkam. There are a thousand families in his village. He estimated that in his village goods worth

Rs 50 lakh every month were being consumed, of which 80 per cent could be manufactured in the village. Soap, oil, bricks, etc., can all be made in the village. So why not do so? If there is an untied fund, people can set up factories in the village, and if all these things are manufactured in the village itself, unemployment and poverty can be eradicated.

There is a successful experiment going on in a block comprising a few villages near Pune. Earlier, these villages would literally starve from June to September. During this time people would either go off to towns or borrow money from moneylenders at an interest rate of 150 per cent. So if they borrowed 100 kilos of grain from the lender, they had to pay 150 kilos as interest after four months. Apart from this, whenever the moneylender would summon them, they would have to leave their work and go to work on his land free of cost. This affected their farming too. They also had to give all the firewood from their land to the moneylender for free.

An organization started a grain bank there. The bank formed a committee of the local people and after gauging the requirement, gave them the requisite food grain on credit. This committee gives loans to needy families. After four months any family is required to return 125 kilos of foodgrains against the 100 kilos borrowed. And all this without the involvement of a moneylender. In four years' time, a village returns the entire loan taken from the organization. After this, every year, the committee has ample food grains. This experiment has been running successfully in about 150 neighbouring villages. If there is an untied fund, it would be possible to start such a grain bank in every village. This would get rid of hunger as well as the moneylender.

The country can be revolutionized if all the government schemes are put to an end and an untied fund is provided to the villages directly. Unemployment and poverty can be eradicated.

WILL EMPOWERING GRAM SABHAS INCREASE CORRUPTION?

Some people believe that if the gram sabhas directly receive an untied fund, it can be misused. Our question is: how? So some people gave an example saying, suppose there is a grant of Rs 3 crore and everybody in the gram sabha meeting decides that they want to divide it amongst themselves and pocket it. But what is wrong with that? Let them divide it amongst themselves and pocket it. Who is pocketing that money at present? The corrupt officials and leaders, the BDO, the tehsildar and the collector. What is wrong if the entire village is taking that money? At least it is reaching the people it is meant for.

But the people of the village will never do such a thing. Who loves a child more—its parents or the education secretary? So, if the parents are participating in the gram sabha, will they say, 'Do not make a school for my child?' or 'Do not make a health centre for my child?' or 'We don't require any of these things, let us all divide the money and pocket it?' This is never going to happen. The people in the village will be worried about different facets of their lives. They will spend on education, health care and roads. It is sheer imagination to think that they will pocket all the money.

The other possible misuse is that the sarpanch does not convene a gram sabha meeting, gets fake signatures from the people and pockets all the money from the untied fund. This is certainly possible. But this is happening even today. If the sarpanch is corrupt he will make his money irrespective of whether the money is in an untied fund or not. Some people believe that 'at least some people are getting the money through schemes'. This is completely wrong. How much money reaches the people in villages depends entirely on how corrupt the sarpanch is and how aware the people of the village are. Wherever people raise their voices they receive the money meant for them. Wherever people raise their voices the untied fund will reach them in larger quantities. Wherever the sarpanch is less corrupt, the untied funding will be larger. Today, the people who are interested in stopping the money from being stolen by corrupt officials are the ones who are likely to benefit most from these schemes. The rest of the people couldn't care less. For example, suppose under the Indira Awaas Yojna, there is a grant of money for three houses. If the sarpanch were to pocket all this money or take a bribe from the three persons for this, the rest of the village wouldn't bother. No one will raise their voice. The ones to suffer will be these three. But if there is an untied fund, the whole village will be involved and the entire village will look into it. Therefore, we believe that because of an untied fund, the entire village will be united in fighting corruption and will be involved in the expenditure of that money. Second, today the people can take no action against a corrupt sarpanch or a corrupt officer. In swaraj (self-governance), the gram sabha would be able to punish them and, if necessary, dismiss them from service.

PEOPLE SHOULD BE CONSULTED ON RULES AND LAWS

According to the Constitution of our country, legislators and parliamentarians are the ex-officio members of the panchayat at the block and district levels. But in the Constitution or in any law they have no responsibilities in this regard. According to us, if any law is presented in Parliament it should be their duty to bring a copy of that proposal to the blocks and districts. And copies of the proposed law should be distributed in the gram sabhas and their opinions taken. People will debate it and the legislator or the parliamentarian should then present in Parliament whatever the outcome and final decision of the debate is. He should be made to present that view in Parliament and declare that it is the view of the people of his area.

Today we choose a legislator or a parliamentarian. We vote for them. They are our representatives. They are first the representatives of the people and then the representatives of the Congress or the BJP or any other party. But they do not ask our opinion about any issue that they vote for in Parliament. All Congressmen vote as Sonia Gandhi dictates. The BJP members vote according to what Advani and Gadkari say. Mayawati orders her partymen to vote as she wants. The people we choose are ordered about by their parties and we have no say.

We have to stop the high-handedness of the 'high command'. Legislators and parliamentarians should be echoing our opinions in Parliament and that is the only way to have direct control over the lawmaking process.

It will then be impossible for Parliament to pass something like the 'nuclear liability' bill. It will be difficult for the government to bow to pressures from foreign governments and foreign companies. Then, the government will have to make laws that the people want.

CONTROL OVER NATURAL RESOURCES

People should have direct control over water, forest, land, minerals and other natural resources.

Land

As we mentioned earlier, a company wanting to set up a factory in any village has to take permission from the state government. In the state government, some minister or official takes a bribe and sells off the village land to these moneyed people. The farmers are not even asked if they wish to farm or sell their land.

There should be changes in the law so that if a company wishes to set up a plant, it should seek the approval of the gram sabha rather than the state government. It should apply to the panchayat secretary of the villages to be affected. The panchayat secretary will then put up the proposal before the gram sabha and the people will decide whether they wish to give their land or not, and if they do, on what conditions. These conditions too should be decided in the gram sabha meeting. If the demands and conditions are acceptable to the company, it can then buy the land.

Similarly, if the Central or state government wishes to acquire land, it should requisition the gram sabha and talk to them directly.

There are many villages where only 10-15 per cent of

the people own land. The others are all labourers on that land. When the land is sold, the money goes to the landlord and those who work on that land get nothing. The gram sabha should think about their welfare before taking a decision. As such, the gram sabha should have direct control of the village land.

Mine/Quarry

The gram sabha should have ownership of small minerals. Who should have the ownership of the richer minerals? Undoubtedly, the whole country should have the right to minerals—no one can object to this. How can we ensure that they are used for the well-being of all? Today, permits for mining are issued by the state and Central governments. In some instances, they have misused this right and have sold the mines for mere pennies after being bribed.

Should the authority to grant permits then be given to the gram sabhas? Some people are of the opinion that mining companies are so strong that they will easily be able to pressurize the village people.

The solution lies in a middle path. The policy for mining, use and export of minerals should be formulated after discussions at the gram sabha level. And the gram sabhas should decide on granting mining permits as per this policy.

Forest

The gram sabha should have direct ownership of the small products from the forest. No contract for timber or bamboo should be given out without the approval of the gram sabhas. The gram sabha should formulate its own terms and conditions.

Water

The gram sabha should have direct ownership of all water bodies in its jurisdiction. Policy decisions regarding the bigger water sources such as rivers should not be taken without consulting the gram sabha.

DISTRIBUTION OF WORK AT VARIOUS LEVELS IN THE GOVERNMENT

It is important to divide the work, government wealth and organizations amongst the various levels in the government. There is a division of work between the state and Central governments but there is no division of labour between the different levels of a state government and the panchayats.

All decisions pertaining to the village should be taken in the gram sabha. First, the people of the village should decide what they want done in the village. Which of the governmental resources, such as roads, drains, etc., fall completely under the purview of their village? Which are the government agencies that serve only their village? Which school teaches only the children of their village? Then all the work, resources and organizations of this type should be handed over to the gram sabha through enactment of a law. The responsibility of executing these tasks, taking care of assets, and the daily functioning of organization should be lawfully handed over to the panchayat.

First and foremost, every village should make such a list. Then every block should make a list of the work, resources and the agencies that are dealing with two or more villages. Next, whatever resources, work or agencies are related to two or more blocks should be put in the district list and whatever relates to two or more districts should go in the state list. Once this is done, the responsibility of the work, resources and agency should be given to the level under which it falls in the list as mentioned above. If there is a dispute between two villages regarding some work, resources or agency, it should be dealt with at the block level. Block-level disputes should be handled at the district level and district-level disputes can be resolved at the state level.

HOW WILL DECISIONS BE TAKEN UNDER THE SYSTEM OF SWARAJ?

The pradhans of all the villages of a block will form a block panchayat. The heads of all blocks will form a district panchayat.

For issues that affect three or four villages—for example, the construction of a road that runs through four villages—decisions will be taken at the block level but the affected villages will be asked to give their opinion in gram sabha meetings. No decisions will be taken at the block level without the permission and agreement of the concerned gram sabhas. If decisions are to be taken with respect to four or five districts, they will be taken at the state level. No decision will be taken at the district level without the permission and agreement of the concerned villages.

To get any work done at the state level, the state government will not require permission from the gram sabhas. The gram sabhas, however, have the right to raise any issue. If more than 5 per cent of the gram sabhas in the state propose a bill to the government, the state government will have to send the bill to all the gram sabhas. If more than 50 per cent of the gram sabhas support that bill, the state government will be oligated to pass it even if it requires amendment of the law.

THE EFFECT OF SWARAJ ON INDIAN POLITICS

The day there are regular gram sabha meetings in all the villages in this country, gram sabhas will have direct control over Parliament. It is then that the tight grip of corrupt politicians and criminals will slacken, people will have power and we will progress.

When people will have direct power, there will be democracy in this country. If that happens, education will improve, health care will improve, there will be roads, water and electricity, and we will be able to put an end to poverty, unemployment and Naxalism.

NEED FOR EXTENSIVE CHANGES IN PANCHAYATI RAJ AND OTHER LAWS

There are many suggestions at the end of this book that can be used by the state and the Central governments to amend and implement the panchayati raj and other laws. It is not necessary to amend the Constitution for this.

SWADESI ISLANDS OF SWARAJ

In ancient India, people used to take governmental decisions. In modern times, the same is happening in many countries. However, few people know whether there are any examples of direct democracy in our country at present. Everyone wrongly feels that it is not possible in our country, but there have been many successful experiments with direct democracy through local leadership. These experiments have brought about many positive changes. Let us look at some examples.

HIVRE BAZAAR IN MAHARASHTRA

Hivre Bazaar is a village in the district of Ahmednagar, about 100 kilometres from Pune. This village faced innumerable droughts from 1972 to 1989. People left the village and went to Pune or Mumbai. Around 90 per cent of its population slipped below the poverty line. The situation was so bad that every house was brewing and consuming alcohol. People were uneducated and poor. There was so much antagonism and rivalry that there had been several murders and the police would visit the village every week. The village had become a hotbed of crime.

In 1989, about twenty to thirty boys from the village got together and decided to change their village. Things could not continue as they were. They chose one amongst them. His name was Popatrao Pawar. They asked him to be the sarpanch of the village. The boy was doing his MCom from Mumbai and he was called back from there. The boys then met the head of every group in the village and requested them to make this boy the sarpanch of the village for a year and promised them that they would change the situation. All the elders laughed at these boys but nonetheless agreed to let the boy be the sarpanch for a year.

The only decision that boy took was that 'I will not take any unilateral decision. Whatever decision has to be taken, I will take in consultation with the entire village.' According to the law, there need to be only two gram sabha meetings in a year—one on 15 August and the other on 26 January. He started having four meetings a month. Whenever there was a problem he would get the whole village together and ask them for solutions and suggestions.

The results were miraculous. In 1989, the per capita income in the village was Rs 840 and today it is Rs 28,000. This means that if there are five members in any family the annual income of the family is approximately Rs 1.5 lakh. This is more than enough money for life in a village!

The village has good roads now. Earlier, people lived in slums, now they have good homes. There is a proper school and hospital, and there is no black marketing of subsidized rations. When the ration arrives, it is offloaded in everyone's presence. Earlier, households were brewing alcohol and now no one drinks alcohol, let alone brewing it. No police case has been registered in the village in the last five years.

Most importantly, Popatrao Pawar, who had been chosen sarpanch for a year, became so popular through his work that twenty years later he is still the sarpanch. No one has been able to defeat him. Actually, no one contests against him and he is chosen sarpanch without any opposition every time.

This was possible because the sarpanch decided to do everything with the agreement and permission of all the people of the village.

Popatrao Pawar did another thing. As we said earlier, government schemes turn us into beggars; he put aside all the schemes. In the first gram sabha meeting, he asked what the problems of the village were and what the solutions could be. Some said there was no drinking water. Some said there was no water for irrigation. Some said there was no electricity. Some said there was no school. It was decided that first of all a school had to be made for the children. Popatrao did not write to any government department to make a school in the village.

He asked the gram sabha if there were any vacant houses. Two people stood up. They had two rooms each that were vacant. They offered the rooms. A school was set up in the four rooms. Where would the teachers come from? He did not write to the government to appoint teachers. He told the gram sabha, 'If any young boys are free, could they teach?' Four boys volunteered. They started teaching. The results at the end of one year were good.

Popatrao tells us that when he started the gram sabha meetings, there was so much groupism in the village that people would not even come to the meetings. There was a lot of fighting among various factions. But within a year people felt that the sarpanch was working for their well-being. He had started a school for the children of the village. Slowly people started attending gram sabha meetings.

Owing to numerous droughts the water level in the village had gone down to 80 feet. After discussions, they decided to harvest water and grow trees. Once again, they did not ask for government help. They planted trees and harvested water. From 80 feet the underground water level came up to 15 feet. Earlier, they couldn't manage one harvest and now they were able to get three harvests.

There is a very interesting anecdote. The forest department had planted trees here in 1980. The people in the village had chopped those trees because they were not theirs and they felt nothing for them. But when it came to cutting the trees they had planted, they didn't allow any one to do so. These were their own. This is how the village developed.

After hearing the story of Hivre Bazaar, many people say that this village progressed because the sarpanch was good. Had Popatrao not been there, this village would not have progressed.

Who is a good sarpanch? We met many sarpanches who are good and honest. They do not make any money on the sly. We met a very good sarpanch in Rajasthan. He is very rich and would spend his own money. But he never consulted the people on anything and never fulfilled their demands. He worked of his own will. He spent his own money and built toilets on the outskirts of the village. But people did not want toilets, and these have been lying locked and unused ever since they were built.

A good sarpanch, therefore, is one who takes decisions in consultation with the people of the village. He implements the decisions taken by the people; only then will he be called a good sarpanch.

But our panchayati raj system today does not give any such authority to the gram sabhas. So, wherever there are good and honest sarpanches, they surrender to the people and declare that they will not take any unilateral decisions and only implement what the people decide. Therefore, in such places there is development but wherever the gram sabha has no say in decision making there is no progress.

We want this type of politics to change. This politics of everything being centred on a good sarpanch has to change.

The day the law is passed to give power directly to the people, there will be no need to wait for a good sarpanch. We will not have to wait for a Popatrao to be born in our village. Irrespective of whether the sarpanch is good or bad, the people will get their work done. They will set their gram sabha in order because then the people will lawfully have the authority to take their own decisions.

AN EXAMPLE FROM A VILLAGE IN NORTH KERALA

What will be the advantage of giving the gram sabha, that is to say, the people, the authority to take decisions? We will try and understand this through an example from Kerala. Under the panchayati raj system in Kerala, no factory can be set up in any village without the permission of the gram sabha. A multinational company wanted to set up a wood factory in north Kerala. If they were to set up this plant, a lot of trees from the area would be chopped but the people of the area did not want the trees to be cut. The company managed to get permission for the plant from the state government, from the minister, from the collector. Even the village headman gave in under pressure. But when the matter reached the gram sabha, they refused to give permission because they cared about their trees.

It is very clear from the example that the government, the minister or the collector can be bought; even the headman can be pressurized, but it is impossible to buy out an entire gram sabha. This is a matter of their lives and they only look to see how their lives can become better.

THE MIRACLE OF A NEW LAW IN MADHYA PRADESH

In 2002, the panchayati raj law in Madhya Pradesh was amended to the effect that if a government worker at the village level was not working well, the people could get together in a gram sabha meeting and stop his salary. This gave rise to many positive results. Some of them are listed below.

We went to a few villages in the Amarwada block of Chhindwara district. Earlier, teachers in the school there would not come to work. They would come on the last day of the month, take their salaries and leave. When this law came into force, the people of the village got together in a meeting of the gram sabha and stopped the salaries of these teachers. They did not get their salaries for two months, and so the third month they got back to school and started teaching. Such a simple solution. Give power to the people and they will progress.

Similarly, we went to another village in Madhya Pradesh. The anganwadi worker there was very irregular. One day the sarpanch got the whole village together and asked the anganwadi worker to come too. In front of all the people he asked her, 'Tell us, how many times have you come in the last six months?' She could not lie in front of the whole village. She accepted that she had come for only two days in the last six months. Then he asked her, 'So if you came for two days only what happened to the money the government sends for the anganwadi centre?' She accepted that she had pocketed all the money.

It is important to realize that if the gram sabha had not had such authority lawfully, they would not have been able to do anything. The anganwadi worker was not coming, she had pocketed all the money, but what could the people have done? They would have only had the option of complaining to the anganwadi director. Their complaint would have been thrown in the dustbin or, if he was a good officer, he would have constituted an enquiry. The investigating officer would have gone to the village, taken a bribe from the anganwadi worker and would have written a report that she had been coming regularly for six months. These complaints have no meaning; they are discarded. Afterwards, the village people would have kept protesting, but who would listen?

When the people in the village were given direct power, the authority to take decisions, no investigation was required. Within no time the woman accepted that she had come only twice in the last six months and had pocketed the money. And as soon as she accepted her crime, some boys stood up and said that the woman should be removed. Then some elders stood up. They said that their aim was not to remove her. They wanted her to change. They said they would give her ten days and if she changed in ten days, fine, else the gram sabha would be reconvened and a decision to remove her would be taken. The woman mended her ways. She did not have to be removed.

WHEN THE PEOPLE WILL DECIDE

If there is swaraj, if people are given direct power under the law, what are the possibilities of development in various sectors? The possibilities of development will increase in all sectors. Given below are a few examples.

IMPROVEMENT IN EDUCATION

The condition of government-run schools, especially in villages, is abysmal at present. Teaching is poor; there are no desks for students to sit, no fans, no toilets and no arrangement of drinking water. And whenever people register a complaint with the government, no action is taken.

If the government makes untied funds available from the top, members of the gram sabha will be able to decide on the amenities to be made available in schools and take decisions directly. They will not have to seek permission from any official, minister or the state government.

Similarly, there is a shortage of teachers in government-run schools. A single teacher handles 200–300 students, and combines two to three classes together. This is not education, but a joke.

Even the teachers who have been assigned duties do

not teach properly. They come only at the end of month and take the salary; or even if they come to the school, they do not teach the students but sit under a tree and gossip, while the children play about. If the gram sabha has the power and the authority, people will be able to summon these teachers, question them and, if necessary, mete out punishment. The power to rectify the behaviour of such teachers will be with the gram sabha.

IMPROVEMENT IN HEALTH CARE

Similarly, let us look at the issue of health care. Doctors in village hospitals do not treat patients properly, hurl abuses at them, act insolently, and do not even come to the hospital. Medicines are stolen. If the gram sabha has the powers, it will be able to summon such doctors directly and demand an explanation and, if necessary, punish them. If there is a short supply of medicines in the hospital, and the gram sabha has access to untied funds, it can even purchase medicines for the hospital. And if medicines are being stolen, it can directly question the hospital staff and punish them. This will directly reduce corruption, as no action is taken against corrupt officials at present.

FREEDOM FROM NAXALISM

By giving powers to the gram sabha, Naxalism will be strongly impacted. Let's try to understand it with an example. A steel company wanted to set up a plant in Lohanigunda in Chhattisgarh. For that purpose it needed land in ten villages. These ten villages are scheduled areas and fall under PESA (Panchayat [Extension to Scheduled Areas]) Act. According to this act, if the government wants to acquire any land, it will have to hold discussions with the gram sabha of the region. The government wrote to the gram sabha conveying their intent, but people refused to give the land. The government requested again and sabhas were reconvened. The sabhas presented the government with sixteen demands and agreed to give the land only if the demands were met. These demands were very reasonable. The villagers sought a certain amount as compensation, talked about a certain number of trees to be planted if trees were felled and sought guarantee of employment for one member of each household. But when the government was sent these demands, it apparently rejected them and acquired the land by using police force. Following this, the villagers painted the village walls with slogans saying 'Naxalites come. Save us'. Later, it became known that the ten villages had joined the Naxalites.

So if the people have the right to take a final decision about their village, they will neither go to the Naxalites nor will they support them. And, without any support base, Naxalism will not survive.

SUCCESS AGAINST ALCOHOLISM

In many wards of Delhi, mohalla sabhas are being held for the past one year. Every month, community members, local officials and politicians meet and discuss the issues of development in the area. In one such community meet in Sonia Vihar, a boy raised an issue saying: 'The liquor shop is very far from our area and it should also open in our colony.' A discussion ensued on the topic. The interesting point to note is that many people sitting in the meet themselves had a habit of drinking, but everybody acts holy in a public place. So, one by one, every person surmised that liquor is a bad thing and the shop should not open in the locality. Thus, the proposal was rejected. That day it became clear that it is very difficult to get a bad proposal passed in a local meet.

At present, to open a liquor shop, one only needs approval from the local politician and an official of the state government, but nobody asks the public. So the politician and the official give the approval, either after taking a bribe or under some pressure. If a law is passed, stipulating that a liquor shop can be opened in a locality only after seeking approval from the community or gram sabha of the region, opening a liquor shop will become a very difficult task. This will be an effective way to combat alcoholism.

SOLUTION TO END POVERTY, HUNGER AND UNEMPLOYMENT

If power is vested in the hands of the people, it will directly impact the problems of unemployment and poverty. As we have written earlier in this book, if untied funds are made available to villages, people will sit in gram sabha meetings and take decisions regarding the poor amongst them, serve their needs, provide them with ration, ensure that nobody remains hungry, provide shelter to all and ensure that all children attend school.

If somebody wants to start a business, the gram sabha will be able to lend money from surplus free funds and help the person start the venture. At present, the villager takes money from a moneylender at an interest of 150 per cent and remains entangled in that trap for his whole life.

Farmers are committing suicide in the country as they are unable to repay the money they borrow from moneylenders. The gram sabha will be able to give loans to such farmers.

If untied funds are made available to a gram sabha, it can open a soap factory, an oil mill, a rice mill, a flour machine and different kinds of industries to support the needs of villagers. These industries will also provide employment to people and alleviate poverty.

Hence, provision of free funds to a gram sabha is a single-step solution to increase the income of an individual and thereby alleviate poverty and check unemployment.

BASELESS FEARS AND MISCONCEPTIONS

People raise all kinds of doubts when there is talk of giving direct power to the people. We have tried to address all these misgivings here.

ATROCITIES ON DALITS

Many people are doubtful about power being given in the hands of the gram sabhas as they fear this will escalate violence against Dalits. To find the answer to this question, we visited a few Dalit colonies in Bihar, educated them about swaraj, and asked them whether they believed that violence against Dalits would increase if more power was given to gram sabhas. Dalits believe that such a system will improve their lot. At present, if an atrocity is committed against a Dalit, he or she has nowhere to go. What structural support does a Dalit have? None!

The whole system supports the people who exploit—the police, the district collector, the BDO and the tehsildar. They all work as agents of exploiters. If all these people are with the exploiters, where will the exploited Dalit go? Even if all the Dalits of the village come together, the only option available to them is to stage a protest in front of the collector's office. Dalits told us that if the gram sabhas were to be given direct power, and all the Dalits were to come together, they would be able to raise their issues in the gram sabha meetings and wage a struggle to get justice. Second, there are many upper-caste people who sympathize with Dalits and want to support them. But in the present system, they are unable to do anything as nobody pays heed to them. So they have no role in the current system. In a gram sabha, such people will also be able to raise their voices and support the Dalits. This is what Dalits told us during our talks.

Besides this, swaraj or self-rule will also open up a new avenue for Dalit struggle. In the new system, a Lokpal will be institutionalized. If people from any village are being stopped from attending a gram sabha meeting, or their grievances are not being heard, they will be able to register a complaint with the Lokpal. And it will be the responsibility of the Lokpal to convene a special gram sabha under his/her watch and make sure that all the people are allowed to attend it.

It is not that the condition of Dalits will improve all of a sudden. Our point is that in what scenario are there more chances of misuse of power: when the whole political power rests with the sarpanch, or when the power is given to the gram sabha? We believe that if the power lies with the gram sabha, the chances of exploitation are comparatively less than when it is with the sarpanch.

At least it will be wrong to suggest that empowering the gram sabha will escalate atrocities against the Dalits, as the safeguards presently available to them will remain intact.

THE FEAR OF KHAP PANCHAYATS

A few people cite the example of khap panchayats—that due to their judgements, there have been cases of girls or boys being killed. So just like the khap, can't the gram sabha take a wrong decision?

It is a matter of contention whether the khaps have given such judgements, but without getting into the debate, we would like to reiterate that under the present law, the gram sabhas do not enjoy such powers, and will not be given powers to exterminate a person. Such a decision will be unlawful and unbinding, as under the scheme mentioned the gram sabhas will function under the Constitution and law of the land. To get somebody killed, amputated, or hung is against the law. Nobody has the right to take anybody's life.

If this is the case, a gram sabha may declare itself to be a separate state from India. Such powers will not rest with the sabha. They will work under the constitutional framework and will work according to the powers bestowed upon them.

WILL SOCIAL EVILS DECREASE OR INCREASE BY EMPOWERING GRAM SABHAS?

What impact will empowering gram sabhas have on social evils such as dowry and child marriage? If the gram sabhas are empowered, will the practice of these evils increase?

All social evils are a result of beliefs that are centuries old. These beliefs control the hearts and minds of the people and many of them have been declared offences punishable under law. So, if any gram sabha was to support any social evil, it would be unlawful.

While the chances of social evils getting strengthened courtesy gram sabhas are minimal, the chances of such evil being rooted out are also remote. We have to understand that if we want to root out these social evils, widespread social movements need to be started and mass dialogue processes initiated so as to clear age-old beliefs from the hearts and minds of the people.

WILL PEOPLE ENGAGE IN FIGHTS IN GRAM SABHAS?

Many people believe that villagers cannot take decisions as they are illiterate, and that if there is a gram sabha, people will clash. Many people reason that if in a sarpanch election, a person secures 60 per cent votes, 40 per cent are against him/her. Such voters will create problems in the organizing of gram sabhas. The global experience, however, shows that such fears are unfounded.

This book gives an example of Hivre Bazaar, where factionalism and fights were rampant; there were murders even. When the gram sabhas started, only a few people used to participate but the number increased over time. The issue of clashes was also discussed and villagers came together to form a platform, and now, Hivre Bazaar is completely self-reliant.

Mohalla sabhas are being held in Delhi for the past one year and people from various walks of life attend these meetings. People from both the Congress and the BJP come. Discussions take place, debates ensue, views and counterviews are exchanged, even fights take place, but decisions are reached finally.

If nothing else happens, at least in those villages where people sit down and take decisions, there will be change. The villages where people have disputes will not see any improvement. Then people won't be able to claim that an official, a party or a politician is corrupt. They will have to accept that they themselves are useless, that they engage in fights, and that unless they rectify themselves, the situation will not improve. They will have only themselves to blame for their fate, their life, poverty and unemployment.

In the present system, an official sitting in Delhi, Lucknow or Bhopal takes decisions about our lives. If we are thirsty and need water, that official sitting far away says that a park will be made, or computers will be provided. How will the official understand our requirements? So it does not matter if we have fights or disagreements in our villages and communities. Decisions regarding the people should be taken at a local level. Only then will we benefit from any decision.

WHAT HAPPENED TO THE PESA ACT?

Many people contend that the PESA has already given lots of power to gram sabhas. Are gram sabhas in tribal areas, where the act is applicable, working fine? Is there any kind of visible improvement in those areas? No.

Not at all!

Even in such areas, gram sabhas are powerless and non-functional. This is because PESA only allows partial powers to gram sabhas. State governments have not even extended full rights under PESA to the gram sabhas.

For example, according to PESA, development policies are to be formulated in gram sabhas. This means that the expenditure of public funds is to be with the gram sabhas. According to the statistics available, the money coming to villages is routed through policies made in Delhi. There is no provision for untied funds, and all issues related to money, including how much is to be spent in a village and on what scheme, are discussed in Delhi and the state capitals. So how do villagers make schemes for their villages? Isn't it interesting that villagers have been given the right to spend money, but not the money itself? Also, under PESA, the gram sabha has been given no control over any village-level government official. It does not hold any power over the village teacher, forest officer, police, tehsildar, or health officer. If these officials do not comply with the sabha's decision, it has no right to punish them. All the officials are affiliated directly to the state government. Often, these officials do not follow the decisions taken by the sabhas, work for the state governments and commit atrocities against the villagers.

Also, in PESA, it has been mentioned that the state government will hold talks with the gram sabha before any land acquisition takes place. In most instances, it has been noticed that talks have been reduced to a mere formality and land is acquired forcibly by sending the police force.

PESA is better than the Panchayat Raj Act, but as long as decisions regarding public funds, government officials and natural resources are not given to gram sabhas, the dream of swaraj/self-rule will be a mere dream.

GOVERNANCE WILL IMPROVE WITH THE PARTICIPATION OF GOOD PEOPLE

Many people believe that electing good people as MLAs, MPs and their representatives will have an impact upon the issues and solve the problems of their area. Such thinking is entirely wrong.

It is essential to understand the role of an MLA or MP

in our system. According to the Constitution, an MLA is a member of the legislative assembly, whereas an MP is a member of Parliament.

If, in our locality, there is no electricity or water supply, roads are not well maintained, sewage is not disposed of and poverty and unemployment are on the rise, we approach an MLA or MP to intervene. But we will have to understand that MPs and MLAs have no power to solve such problems. According to the Constitution, these issues do not fall under the purview of their responsibilities. According to the Constitution, an MLA is supposed to get good laws passed in the assembly and an MP is supposed to get good laws passed in the Parliament. If the government machinery is not working properly in an area, an MLA or MP cannot help in any manner. The Constitution or law does not give them any power to deal with such problems. Thus, if the road in our area has potholes, or the fair-price shop owner is not distributing ration properly, the MLA or MP cannot initiate any action against the engineer or the ration shopowner but can only raise a question in the Parliament or assembly. Now, if every MLA and MP wants to raise questions, it results in a flood of questions in the House or assembly. In such a scenario, a lottery is used to select which MLA or MP can ask the question. So despite his/her best effort, your MP or MLA cannot raise all your concerns in the Parliament or assembly.

An MLA or MP also gets a fund of Rs 2 crore and it is expected that she or he will use it for development projects in the area. But they can only give permission to carry out the projects and do not hold any control over their satisfactory completion. Such a right rests with the officials under various departments and an MP or MLA does not wield any power over these officials. It is said that MPs and MLAs take bribes while assigning a certain development project; but even if the work is not being done properly, they do not have the authority to stop the payment or get it rectified.

It is the duty of the MP and the MLA to get good laws passed. But unfortunately, it is not so easy. Whenever any bill is presented in the House, each political party issues an order to either support or reject the bill and he or she has to toe the party line. An MLA or MP cannot even vote in favour or against any bill according to his or her will.

So it is clear that neither can they help solve our daily problems, nor can they help in getting good laws passed. This is the dichotomy of the situation. We elect them, but they act according to the wishes of the party they belong to. And if they don't toe the party line, they are punished and may even have to lose their membership of the House or assembly.

So even if you elect a good or honest person as an MLA or MP from your area, it will neither solve the issues ailing your area, nor will he or she be able to help pass a good law. Isn't it a queer democracy, where neither the public is heard nor its representatives? Only a few people—ministers, chief ministers or the prime minister—wield the power; and though we elect them, these few people, along with officials, run the country for five years. Neither do the people have any control over the system, nor do the elected representatives. Can such a democracy safeguard our rights? Should we feel proud about such a democracy?

In Mirchpur village of Haryana, Dalits were treated in an inhuman way. Over seventy MPs in our Parliament belong to SC and ST categories. These seats are reserved to safeguard the rights of SCs and STs. When atrocities were committed against Dalits in Mirchpur, naturally the question that came to mind was, why was the issue not raised by these MPs in the House? Later, a few MPs disclosed that they could not do anything without the consent of the party. So has our democracy got stuck in the internal politics of parties?

We agree with people who say that we should elect good people, but merely electing good people will not improve the system; it will only stop or slow down the process of political deterioration.

At present, the system is so distorted that an honest minister or officer is not able to do anything. His/her superiors, juniors and colleagues do not allow him to work properly. Many an honest official has been heard saying: 'We agree with your concerns and the issue you have raised is valid. But we have pressure from the top and will not be able to help you.'

ANY POLITICAL CHANGE IS IMPOSSIBLE WITHOUT REFORMS

In our country, a lot of good people and good institutions work on different issues such as education, health care, water, forests and land. We have to understand that unless the whole political system is changed, and decision-making power is vested in the hands of the public, these issues will remain unresolved. Even if we use our entire power to change the laws related to these issues, the executive power will still lie with the collector, and if he or she does not implement the policy properly, what chance will we have against that official? This is how things have been in our country. Good laws are made and flouted. If the officials who are supposed to implement the laws flout them, nothing can be done.

So until the gram sabha is given the power to summon the officials not performing their duties, the problems in areas of education, health care, water, forests and land will not ease. We have to understand that unless we strike at the root, real change is not possible.

CHARACTER BUILDING AND STRUCTURAL REFORMS

Many people believe that we should invest more in building good human character. If people change for the better, the system will improve itself.

But has the present system become so corrupt as to stop character building?

The biggest problem today is that the present system does not allow character building. However hard a person tries, he or she cannot be honest. So, is character building possible without restructuring the present system?

Let us understand this through an example. The commission that fair-price and kerosene oil shopowners get is so little that without indulging in malpractices they cannot earn a living. On one litre of kerosene, a commission of 7 paisa is earned. With a quota of 10,000 litres, the maximum monthly income of the shop owner is Rs 700. Besides paying rent for the shop, he has to also support his family, which is impossible with this kind of money. Will such a person not indulge in malpractices? Delhi has about 4,000 fair-price shops, so effectively by introducing a wrong system, the government has corrupted 4,000 people. So till the time the government increases the commission, how can one expect honesty from these fair-price traders? Till the time the system is changed, how is character building possible?

Why are we talking about character or system building

here? The highest aim of human life has been thought to be the attainment of nirvana/Buddhatva by conquering one's desires and limitations. So character building is the aim of life and nature. A good system allows the formation of good character and a bad system impedes it. There is no doubt that as and when character building happens, the system will improve too, and as and when the system improves, character building will gain pace. To walk on a righteous path and fight for justice and help in the formation of a just system are the highest goals of human life. By attaining such goals, character building becomes stronger.

At present, we see that many politicians, officials and traders indulge in malpractices. But most of these people do so because of a corrupt system. If we give them a good system, won't many of them correct themselves? So, both character building and system formation are essential.

LET THERE BE A LAW
FOR SELF-RULE

Changes will have to be made in our laws so that people can take direct decisions through the gram sabhas. This is important to ensure that people have control over their lives and destiny and take responsibility for their own development. We propose the following changes:

THE GRAM SABHA SHOULD BE SUPREME

Problem: In the existing system, the panchayats have very limited authority. Whatever little power they have is controlled by the sarpanch (mukhiya or pradhan). The gram sabha has no power over the sarpanch. They have been made appendages to the sarpanch. In most of the panchayati laws, the role of the gram sabha is limited to advising the sarpanch, which he or she may heed or ignore. As a result, many of the sarpanches are corrupt. People helplessly watch the corruption that takes place in panchayats. They cannot do anything about it. And that is also the reason that people stay away from the working of panchayats and gram sabhas.

The law does not allow the people to do anything if the sarpanch is corrupt or does something wrong. The district magistrate is authorized to act against him. But there are more than a thousand panchayats under the purview of a district magistrate who sits in the district headquarters quite far from the villages. How is it possible for him to know if the sarpanch is honest or corrupt? Most of the time, no action is taken against a sarpanch when people complain against him because the district magistrate just doesn't have the time. In case the sarpanch belongs to the party in power or is close to the local MLA or MP, the district magistrate takes no action against him under duress. Therefore, no action is taken against corrupt sarpanches anyway.

In fact, corruption is prevalent at the district magistrate level too. Many sarpanches are harassed by having false charges registered against them. The district magistrate has many villages under him so he normally puts the BDO or some such official in charge of keeping an eye on the sarpanch. These junior officers start demanding money from the sarpanches. Those who don't pay face false charges. Quite often the officials force the sarpanches to commit wrongdoings, and sometimes, under political pressure, they are forced to give false testimony against sarpanches belonging to rival political parties.

Suggestion: First and foremost, the sarpanch has to be liberated from the clutches of the collector and made answerable to the people. We have the following suggestions for this:

(a) The gram sabha should have the authority to take all decisions. The decisions of the gram sabha are final. The sarpanch is only responsible for implementing these decisions.

(b) If the sarpanch is corrupt or found to be involved in illegal activities, the gram sabha should be able to order the police to lodge a case against the culprit, and the progress report in the investigation should be presented before the gram sabha at regular intervals.

(c) Till such time as the gram sabha specifically requests it, no action should be taken against the sarpanch by the district magistrate or any other official.

(d) If the sarpanch does not follow the directives of the gram sabha, it should have the authority to recall him. If more than 50 per cent of the voters sign and give a petition to the state election commission, the commission should verify the signatures in fifteen days' time, and within one month of verification, they should have a secret ballot for impeachment. If the no-confidence motion is successful, the sarpanch will be removed from his post and a new election should take place for a new sarpanch.

Recalling the sarpanches is a 'brahmastra' or the ultimate weapon that should be used only as a last resort. Some states have already given the gram sabhas this power.

And some villages have also used it. Unfortunately, the gram sabha does not have any power to deal with situations that fall in the grey area. Either you keep the sarpanch or remove him. There is no system to improve the working of the sarpanch. As soon as the action to remove the sarpanch begins, local politics also starts playing a role. Moreover, people who are not local but have political associations also try and influence the proceedings. This results in an undesirable situation in the village and hinders healthy debate.

We believe that if the gram sabha were to be given powers according to the suggestions mentioned above, the people would be able to keep a check on the sarpanch at regular intervals. Then the sarpanch may not even have to be removed as he would be working with the people according to their wishes. In other words, the brahmastra may never have to be used.

VILLAGE WORK SHOULD BE DONE AT THE LEVEL OF THE GRAM SABHA

Problem: There is confusion as to what work and resources and which organizations come under whose purview.

Suggestion: Which work, what resources and which organization will control what should be listed out and signed (according to the process explained earlier on pages 69-70). After that, all funding should be dealt with by the concerned official.

CONTROL OVER GOVERNMENT WORKERS

Problem: People feel completely helpless before local government employees.

Suggestion:

(a) All workers associated with the work, resources and organizations allocated to the different levels of the panchayats should be responsible to the officials at the respective level. Further, these workers should be considered employees of the panchayat to which they are attached. When one worker retires, the panchayat should directly make the appointment for a replacement. The state government then should not have any role in the appointment.

(b) All panchayats at all levels should have the right to recruit new workers according to their requirements. These people should not be considered state employees but employees of the panchayat.

(c) The panchayat should have complete disciplinary control over its workers, whether they are transferred there or are its direct appointees. In other words, the gram sabha should be able to warn, punish and, if required, remove its workers from their posts.

(d) The gram sabha should have the right to cancel the licences for government contractors such as the subsidized ration shopkeeper, and appoint whom they find suitable.

(e) All gram sabhas should have the power to issue orders to any worker of their block or district panchayat and, if required, issue summons to him to appear in the sabha. If these orders are not in conflict with the orders of another village, they should be considered obligatory for the concerned officer. In case of a clash of interests, the solution should be sought in a higher appropriate panchayat. If any officer ignores the summons of the gram sabha and/or disregards its orders, the gram sabha should have the right to pull up such an officer or impose a fine on him.

CONTROL OF GOVERNMENT FUNDS

Problem: The Central as well the state governments very often make baseless programmes and schemes that do not have any connection with reality. It has already been discussed in detail how these schemes are promoting corruption, are far removed from the needs of the people, and are making beggars out of people.

Solution: We believe that all these schemes should be stopped. Most of the funds given to the panchayats should be untied. People should decide in gram sabhas how the money should be spent.

The government of Kerala allocates over 40 per cent of its annual budget directly to the panchayats. The need of today is that every state should allocate at least 50 per cent of its annual budget directly to the panchayats in the form of untied funds. There should be no condition attached to this money. The people of the village should be allowed to spend this money as they deem fit.

The panchayats face many problems in trying to get funds released from higher officials and sometimes they have to be bribed as well. Therefore, as it happens in Kerala, the money meant for every panchayat of every level should be credited to their account on 1 April every year. The panchayats should not have to get their money released from anywhere.

In case a Dalit group has a demand in any village, a determined part of the village panchayat fund should be set aside for the Dalit gram sabha keeping in mind the population in the concerned village. This will ensure that the Dalits are not bullied by stronger groups in the village.

CONTROL OF BLOCK AND DISTRICT PANCHAYATS

Problem: In the present system, the village panchayats work under the middle- and district-level panchayats. The middle-level panchayats approve the proposals of the village panchayats and all payments are also made by middle-level and district-level panchayats. The people have no control over the working of these panchayats.

Suggestion: We should form a system in which the village panchayats should not be working under the middle-level and district-level panchayats. Instead, they should be directly controlling them. We propose that through the gram sabhas and pradhans the people should have direct control of the middle-level and district-level panchayats.

(a) The proposal and decision of the gram sabha should be final. They should not need to obtain any kind of administrative, financial or any other permission from above.

(b) The block or district panchayat should be obligated to take the consent of all gram sabhas before starting any new project. Second, any gram sabha has the right to suggest a scheme to the block or district panchayat. Any scheme can only be implemented if all concerned gram sabhas approve of it.

(c) The sarpanch should act as the bridge only between the gram sabha and the block panchayat. Before making any promises in the block panchayat the sarpanch should be obligated to consult his gram sabha and seek their approval. If the gram sabha wishes, it can give the sarpanch a certain degree of autonomy. But this autonomy must be very limited.

DIRECT CONTROL OF POLICYMAKING AND LEGISLATIVE ASSEMBLIES

Problem: India has a representational democracy. Though we choose our leaders we have no control over them between elections. We have no say in the laws enacted by the state or Central governments. In the last few years, some of the laws made by governments have been against the well-being of the people but beneficial to some private companies, national as well as international. It is imperative to put an end to this.

Suggestion: The people should have direct control over the lawmaking process to a certain degree. This control can be given to the people in two ways:

(a) *The role of the people in making new laws or policies:* If 5 per cent or more of the gram sabhas put forth a proposal to frame a law or policy, the state government should send a copy of the proposal to the rest of the gram sabhas. If 50 per cent of all existing gram sabhas accept the proposal, the state government will have to pass that law or implement the policy. And the same would apply to rescind any policy or scheme.

This way the people will be able to directly take the initiative in bringing about improvement in various fields like the police or judiciary. This will give rise to a new phase of improvement.

(b) *People's opinion on all laws and proposals in the Parliament and state legislative assemblies:* According to the Constitution of India, the local legislator and the MP are ex-officio members of the block or the district panchayat. But they have not been assigned any responsibilities in the law. Provisions should be made that they present a copy of all the bills and proposals presented in the Parliament and legislative assembly (barring the financial and no-trust bills) to the block panchayat (or the district council), and that a copy of the proposal be given to all the gram sabhas of the block (or district). There should be a discussion and debate in all the gram sabhas and the MP and legislators should then put forth the consensus opinion of all gram sabhas in the House.

THE RIGHT TO INFORMATION OF THE GRAM SABHA

Problem: The people do not have any information on any decisions of the government that have a direct bearing on their lives.

Solution: The gram sabha should have the right to seek information from any government official up to the state level that concerns their village directly or indirectly. If the concerned officer does not provide the information, the gram sabha should have the right to impose a fine of Rs 25,000 on the concerned officer.

CONTROL OF THE PANCHAYAT SECRETARY

Problem: The state government appoints the panchayat secretary. He, along with the sarpanch and other officers, increases corruption. He is not answerable in any way to the people.

Solution: The gram sabha should appoint the panchayat secretary. He should only be responsible for implementing the decisions of the gram sabha. The gram sabha should have total control over him, from punishing him to stopping his salary and, if required, dismissing him.

CORRUPTION IN PANCHAYATS

Problem: There is rampant corruption in the government. Many a times a bribe has to be paid for paperwork that is of no consequence. People keep complaining but nobody listens. There are two main reasons for this kind of corruption:

(a) Whenever there is any official work undertaken in a village, the officer in charge has to verify that the work has been completed satisfactorily and that payment can be made. The people or the gram sabha are not consulted about this. For example, in Uttar Pradesh, the SDM authenticates that a canal has been cleaned well. Now an SDM who is corrupt takes a bribe and certifies this, even though the canal may not have been cleaned. The farmers who use this canal for irrigating their land are not asked.

(b) When there are complaints against these officers, senior officers of the concerned department carry out the enquiry. They don't take action against these complaints because either they don't care, or are bribed or are under political pressure. And the people have no control over the officers.

Suggestions: In both the cases enumerated above, the following rights should be given to the gram sabha:

(a) Till the gram sabha issues a certificate of satisfaction, no payment should be made for official work. If the gram sabha feels that the work is unsatisfactory, it should have the right to not only stop the payment but also to investigate the reasons for the unsatisfactory work. It should be able to identify the culprits and order them to rectify the shortcomings. If the culprits are in any way associated with the panchayat at any level, the gram sabha should have the authority to take action against them.

(b) If it is a case of criminal corruption, the gram sabha should have the right to order the police to lodge a case and to demand regular updates in the investigations.

ALCOHOLISM IN VILLAGES

Problem: Alcohol shops obtain licences through political connections. The officers often hand out licences under political pressure and take bribes for these. Alcohol stores are creating problems in the villages. Families are being destroyed. The irony is that though people are directly affected by this no one asks them if an alcohol shop should be opened or not. These shops are imposed upon them.

Solution: The licence for an alcohol shop should be granted only if the gram sabha approves it and 90 per cent of the women attending the gram sabha vote in favour of it. The women present in a gram sabha should, through a majority vote, be able to cancel the licence of an alcohol shop.

INDUSTRY AND MINING LICENCE

Problem: Licences for mining and industry are granted by the state or Central governments. The local people have to deal with the repercussions. They do not have any say in the process of granting of these licences.

Solution: No industrial or mining company should be granted a licence without the permission of the gram sabha. The gram sabha should be allowed to lay down its conditions. If the companies violate these conditions, the gram sabhas should have the right to withdraw their permission.

LAND ACQUISITION

Problem: Various state agencies acquire land without the consent of the people. Many people end up losing their homes or employment. Often, compensation is inadequate. Even if compensation is in tandem with the market rates, it does not solve the farmer's problems. A farmer feeds his entire family on one acre of land but the 40,000 rupees (for example) he gets as compensation will not feed his family for life. People are becoming poorer because of land acquisition.

Moreover, the landowners are compensated when the land is acquired but those who work on that land are left unemployed.

In many places, it has been seen that when land was forcibly acquired from the people despite stiff opposition, they joined the Naxal movement.

Solution: The gram sabhas should be empowered to decide whether the project is in favour of the people and whether land should be acquired for the same and, if yes, on what conditions. Amendments should be made in the law to facilitate this.

(a) If a company, a state or the Central government

wishes to acquire land, it should apply to the village panchayat for the same.

(b) Copies of all papers pertaining to the details of the project to be set up on the land, translated into the local language, should be made available to the panchayats of all villages concerned so that people affected can be made aware of all facets of the project.

(c) Panchayats should run an awareness programme on the basis of these papers. If any individual or village wants a copy of the documents, they should be made available at a cost.

(d) On receipt of documents, all panchayats should convene a gram sabha meeting within two months. Every sabha meeting should discuss the project. If there are any queries or doubts, the gram sabha will write to the soliciting company or the state or Central government through its panchayat to provide clarifications and answers in the next meeting of the gram sabha by sending an officer for the same. If more documents are required, the gram sabha can ask for those too.

(e) The people will put forward their questions to the officer sent for clarifications. But no decision will be taken in this meeting about land acquisition. This is only for clearing doubts.

(f) If the gram sabha is satisfied with the answers

provided by the officer and the documents provided, another meeting of the gram sabha will be called to take the final decision. It can also write to the company, state or Central government asking for further details.

(g) No outsider—individual or official—nor the police will be present at the final meeting. Only the media will be allowed to watch from a distance. Such a gram sabha meeting will not be chaired by the sarpanch or the pradhan. The people present will choose a respected person to chair the meeting. The panchayat secretary will not take the minutes of the meeting. This task will be entrusted to somebody from the village. This gram sabha will decide whether the village wants to give its land or not and, if yes, on what conditions. The gram sabha will keep in mind everyone's well-being while trying to arrive at a consensus. The interest of those who will lose their livelihood or are landless will also be kept in mind. If required, a collective gram sabha meeting of more than one village can also be convened so that a consensus can be reached through talks.

(h) The decision of the gram sabha will be final and binding. It cannot be overturned by any government nor can any changes be made to it.

(i) There should be a national resettlement policy that

lays down the minimum rights of the landed as well as the landless people. If a gram sabha agrees to land in the village being acquired by the government, the minimum rights accorded to people in this policy will be the guidelines. But if the gram sabha so wishes, it can ask for more rights than laid down in the policy. The decision of the gram sabha will be final.

(j) There is a serious food shortage in the country at the moment. This problem will only intensify in times to come. It is, therefore, very important that fertile land be used only for farming. The nation can make do without electricity, roads and factories but we cannot survive a day without food. It is important to include in the law that land that has two or more harvests should be marked out by the gram sabha in every village. This land should not be used for anything other than farming under any condition.

LAND DOCUMENTS

Problem: The local government officials tamper with land documents on a large scale. Many cases have come to light wherein land belonging to a poor man has been transferred to someone else without his knowledge. It is also difficult to acquire any information in the offices of land documents and even more difficult to manage to get your work done.

Solution: The panchayat office should be in charge of looking after the documents relating to land under the supervision of the gram sabha. Every month, a list of all sale deeds should be brought out by the gram sabha.

CONTROL OF NATURAL RESOURCES

Problem: For centuries, local people have used natural resources in limited quantities and would take responsibility for their conservation. The control of rivers, forests and mines by the governments started with the British and this practice continued after independence also. In the past few years, there has been a tremendous increase in the exploitation of natural resources by uprooting the local population. As we have mentioned earlier in the book, our natural resources are being sold to contractors and companies.

Solution: The gram sabha should be made the owner of all small water sources, small minerals and small forest products in the areas that fall under its purview. It should also be ensured that without the permission of any affected village, no rights over land, forest or mines would be given away. The gram sabha should decide whether permission should be granted for tapping natural resources and on what terms and conditions. If these conditions are contravened, the gram sabha should have the right to withdraw its permission. In such a case the company will pay for any damage to the environment and society.

As we have said earlier, natural resources are national treasures. Their use should be decided through national policies formulated after discussions in the gram sabhas. Gram sabhas should decide on permission for schemes in their areas.

CORRUPTION IN THE SDM OFFICE

Problem: People have to pay bribes for obtaining certificates.

Solution: The panchayats should issue certificates pertaining to caste, income, domicile, etc. If the panchayat secretary is lax in carrying out this task, he should be questioned in the next meeting of the gram sabha.

TAX COLLECTION

Problem: We have a very unscientific way of collecting taxes and spending the money. Most of the taxes are collected by the Central and state governments and the money is sent to the people through various schemes. There is a leakage at two levels in this method. One, when the money is collected and sent to the top, and second, when the money is sent to the bottom. What is surprising is why some taxes aren't collected and spent locally.

Solution: Experience tells us that if people are actively involved in the collection of taxes and if they understand its benefits, tax collection is very efficient.

Therefore, it is important to involve the gram sabha in the collection of taxes as far as possible. The gram sabha is the single body of the people for whom the tax collection is to be made. Nobody is better suited for collection and expenditure of tax money. We have the following suggestions in this respect:

(a) Taxes which will be levied and collected by the state government.

(b) Taxes which are to be levied by the state government but will be collected by the designated panchayat.

(c) Taxes which will be levied by a higher-level panchayat but will be collected by a lower level as designated by the panchayat.

(d) Taxes which will be levied and collected by one designated level of the panchayat. Try and put maximum tax heads under this list so that all levels of the panchayat are financially autonomous.

Earnings from the property of the gram sabha and taxes collected therefrom should be directly deposited in the account of the panchayat. A part of the tax collected from the market should also be given to the panchayats.

MANY VILLAGES MEETING IN ONE PANCHAYAT

Problem: Far-flung villages are grouped together under one panchayat and because of this people find it difficult to participate in gram sabha meetings. Moreover, these villages are very different from one another. So much so that even neighbouring villages differ in culture, food habits, caste equations, financial situation and resources. Many times these villages have old enmities. Coupled with this, when there is distance between the villages and lack of transport, it is almost impossible for people to participate in the meetings of the gram sabhas.

Suggestion: Every village, however small it may be, should be declared a separate panchayat. Only if two or more villages decide to form a single panchayat should they be merged. The tribal areas have such a provision under law. Non-tribal areas should also have this provision.

CONSTITUTING BLOCK- AND DISTRICT-LEVEL PANCHAYATS

Problem: In the present system, all chiefs of lower panchayats are members of the higher panchayats. Apart from this there is also a general election for some members of the block- and district-level panchayats. Experience has shown that the inclusion of these elected members has not made any difference to the working of the panchayats. In fact, it has only increased corruption. Whenever there is a no-confidence motion against any mid-level or district-level panchayat president, most of the members start auctioning their votes. In many cases the chiefs have to regularly pay these members to stay on in the chair. Moreover, these members spend a lot more money during their elections as compared to the gram sabha mukhiya, as their electoral area is larger. So obviously, after elections, they waste no time in recovering the money with interest.

Suggestion: The practice of election of members to mid- and district-level panchayats should be completely stopped. Only members of panchayats at the lower level should be nominated members of the higher panchayats and only then will the gram sabha be able to control the high-level panchayat through its representatives. So, all sarpanches of one block should be made members of the block panchayat. They can then elect a president amongst them. Similarly, all block presidents should be nominated to the district panchayat and one of them can be elected president. The sarpanch of a village panchayat can work as a mediator between the gram sabha and the block panchayat. He can apprise the block panchayat of the decisions of the gram sabha and vice versa. In this manner, the gram sabha can control what happens at the block level. And using the same logic, the block panchayat presidents can work as mediators between the block panchayat and the district panchayat.

TRANSPARENCY OF DOCUMENTS

Problem: Despite the right to information, it is very difficult to obtain information about the working and decisions of all levels of panchayats. In some areas, where people have sought information about the sarpanches and officers, there are reports of them being harassed. The mukhiya and the police have got together and registered false cases against them and, in some places, there have been attempts on their lives as well.

Suggestion: The documents of the panchayats should be made accessible to bring about transparency in the working of all levels of panchayats. All documents of the village, block and district panchayats should be made public. There should be a system wherein anyone can take a look at these documents without applying for the same. There should be two days in the week fixed for this. If somebody wishes to have a copy of any document, he should be given the same within a week, only charging him the cost of the photocopy. If there is any violation, the gram sabha should have the authority to punish the guilty workers.

ESTABLISHING A LOKPAL

Problem: There is no way in the present system to deal with infringements in the panchayati raj law, or where the gram sabha is not allowed to function properly or if a particular section of society is not being allowed to participate in the gram sabha or if minutes of the gram sabha meeting are not being recorded properly. In such cases, the district magistrate has to take action and he or she is often unfair owing to pressure from local politicians.

Often, people of higher castes in some areas do not allow Dalits to participate in the gram sabhas. If they are allowed to participate, they are not allowed to speak, and if at all they are allowed to speak, their opinions are not recorded in the minutes of the meeting.

Suggestion: We propose that a lokpal should be constituted to deal with such complaints. Such an institution exists in Kerala and the results have been good. We suggest that a lokpal be appointed at the state level as well. He would be responsible for dealing with complaints related to violation of laws related to the panchayati raj law and he should ensure a smooth functioning of the panchayati raj system. His election should be through participation of the people and be completely transparent. He should be provided all resources to be able to work effectively and within time limits. If someone complains that the gram sabha meetings are not being held regularly or that some people are not being allowed to attend them or that the minutes are not being recorded properly, the lokpal should then carry out an investigation and, if the complaint is valid, he should organize a meeting of the gram sabha and ensure that such meetings are held regularly.

STOP INTERVENTION OF THE STATE GOVERNMENT

Problem: Under the existing panchayati raj law, the state governments can issue directives to the panchayats any time and, as a result, the panchayats have turned into inefficient departments of the state government. The sarpanches are busy following the orders of the state government rather than listening to the problems of the people and trying to find solutions to those. Decisions such as the date of the gram sabha meeting, the agenda for the meeting, the organization of various bodies, their responsibilities, etc., are not taken in the village but in the state secretariat. The state tries to control all decisions, even those that have to deal with the everyday lives of the people. As a result, people have forgotten what is expected of them and the panchayats and the gram sabhas have lost their autonomy as well.

Suggestion: The state government should not have the authority to give directives to the panchayats. The panchayats should be considered the third independent body of the administration. If required, the state government at most can advise the panchayats but should not interfere in its day-to-day workings.

CONSTITUTION OF BENEFIT GROUP/COUNCILS

Problem: Suppose in a village of hundred people only ten avail of subsidized ration. If all hundred people are asked their opinion about this system, ninety people would probably say that subsidized ration is not required. This would be a wrong basis to take a decision.

Suggestion: This problem can be solved to a certain extent by the concept of benefit group/councils. Involved in these benefit councils will be those who are directly affected by a particular decision of the gram sabha. In the example given above, the ten people who avail the subsidized ration will form a benefit group. Similarly, if, for example, a gram sabha decides to construct a road, the people living on both sides of that road will form a benefit group. They will decide if the road has been made properly. The decisions of the benefit group meetings will be considered the decision of the gram sabha.

SELF-RULE NECESSARY IN TOWNS TOO

A general meeting of the people of a village is called the gram sabha. Our Constitution says so. Although the Constitution mentions gram sabhas, these have not been given any authority/control. We believe that swaraj means that people should have direct control over government funds, workers, policies, lawmaking processes and natural resources through gram sabhas. Unfortunately, for town dwellers, neither the Constitution nor the law recognizes their general body meetings. A new law will have to be made for this.

DELHI'S EXPERIMENTS

It is true that mohalla sabhas (community meetings) are not yet recognized by law. But citizens have started taking the initiative in many areas. The experiments that have taken place in Delhi in this regard are exemplary. In some areas of east Delhi, community meets are being organized at the initiative of the swaraj campaign, and people are taking official decisions about local issues. Leaders and officials are busy implementing them. This amazing change is taking place in the MCD wards of Trilokpuri and Sunder Nagri. Every ward here has been divided into ten communities. Every community convenes a general meeting every month or two.

Councillors and other local officials are present in all the meetings, where people decide how the corporation's money is to be spent and on what. The situation today is that any member of the mohalla sabha can raise issues related to road, electricity or water. The officials and councillors present in the meeting note the complaint and a fund is allocated for it. If the list for tasks to be done is too long and there are not enough funds to attend to all, the priority of the tasks to be carried out is put to vote immediately.

The councillors of Trilokpuri and Sunder Nagri have declared that the contractors of the area will be paid only when the mohalla sabha declares that it is satisfied with the quality of work done. This has resulted in a big improvement in the quality of work.

The community openly drafts a list of beneficiaries of social security schemes such as the old-age pension, handicapped pension and widow pension. People discuss with complete transparency and honesty who the poorest are and who should benefit from these schemes. Earlier, these benefits went only to the councillors' relatives or close friends.

The lieutenant governor of Delhi has congratulated the councillors who organize mohalla sabhas in their wards. He has also instructed the police to attend the mohalla sabha meetings. He has also asked the commissioner of the municipal corporation to try and organize such mohalla sabhas in other areas in Delhi.

THE CENTRAL GOVERNMENT'S INITIATIVE

There is now a clamour to lawfully recognize mohalla sabhas. Last year, the Centre forwarded to all state governments a draft of a 'Nagar Raj Bill'. They were asked to make amendments in the bill according to their judgements and pass it in their respective legislative assemblies. This was a big step taken by the Central government. For the first time, a new citizen body in towns, called the mohalla sabha, was given due recognition. But the sad part is that the Central government has not given the mohalla sabhas any authority.

Eminent citizens of the country—such as Supreme Court lawyer Prashant Bhushan, social activist Anna Hazare and former chief secretary of Madhya Pradesh, S.C. Bahar—have expressed dissatisfaction with the government's draft and prepared a new draft for the Town Rule Bill. Let us see what the provisions in this new draft are.

PRINCIPAL PROVISIONS OF THE
PROPOSED LEGISLATION

Constitution of mohalla sabhas

(a) A mohalla sabha should be constituted by

putting together 3,000 people of a particular area. If the population of any ward in the town is more than 3,000, numerous mohalla sabhas of 3,000 people each can be formed. All people living in the geographical area of the concerned mohalla sabha should be considered members of the said sabha.

(b) A representative from each mohalla sabha should be elected with the assistance of the state election committee.

(c) All representatives of the mohalla sabha in a ward should then form a ward council. The councillor of the concerned ward should be the chairperson of the ward council.

(d) All issues related to that particular community should be dealt with by the mohalla sabha. Issues related to the ward should be dealt with in the ward council through consultation and dialogue with the mohalla sabha.

(e) The mohalla sabha meetings should be presided over by the representative of the sabha. He has to be the link between the mohalla sabha and the ward committee. He is bound to accept all decisions of the mohalla sabha. He cannot take any decisions without consulting the sabha.

(f) All decisions of the mohalla sabha should be taken in the monthly meeting of the sabha, and if some decision is taken at any place other than the meeting, the decision should be ratified at the mohalla sabha meeting.

Financial control

(a) The ward committee should have independent sources of revenue. The ward committee in its concerned wards should have the authority to levy and collect taxes in certain cases after consultations with the mohalla sabha.

(b) Apart from the locally collected taxes, the ward committees should be given an additional untied fund for development by the municipal corporation, and the state and the Central governments.

(c) The mohalla sabha should decide what work should be carried out where.

(d) The contractor in any community should be paid only after the mohalla sabha issues a certificate of satisfaction for his work.

Control over workers

(a) All decisions of the mohalla sabha should be taken collectively in the mohalla sabha meetings. The elected representative of the mohalla sabha and the local officials are responsible for the implementation of these decisions.

(b) The mohalla sabha should have the right/

authority to recall the representative if he is found to be circumventing their decisions or his work is found unsatisfactory.

(c) The mohalla sabha should have the authority to ask the working junior engineer, principal, manager of the subsidized ration shop, medical supervisor, gardener, and medical superintendent of hospitals of their area to be present in the mohalla sabha meetings.

(d) The mohalla sabha should have the authority to stop the salary or punish the local government officials mentioned in the previous point if they do not heed the summons to attend the meeting or if they are found lacking in their duties. The sabha should not have to seek permission from any other authority to do so.

(e) The mohalla sabha should have the authority to cancel the licence of the ration shop if it is found that the shop is not distributing rations fairly. They should have the authority to award the licence to a new person.

Responsibilities

(a) The mohalla sabhas should ensure that no one in their community is homeless, hungry or uneducated and that everybody has access to adequate medical facilities.

(b) The rights and responsibilities of the ward committees should be the same as those of the mohalla sabhas. All major decisions of the ward committees should have the approval and agreement of the mohalla sabhas for them to be implemented.

(c) The slums in any community should not be removed till their inhabitants are resettled in accordance with official policies. The mohalla sabhas dealing with the certificate of satisfaction should issue the respective certificate in this regard.

(d) Villages in places like Delhi should have full control over their land.

CONTROL OVER MUNICIPALITIES/CORPORATIONS

Any community can ask the concerned municipality or city corporation to consider and decide on any issue by passing a proposal by a two-thirds majority. The municipal corporation would be obligated to consider such a proposal and take a decision on it.

PARTICIPATE IN YOUR GRAM OR MOHALLA SABHA

PARTICIPATE IN YOUR GRAM OR MOHALLA SABHA

Whenever there is talk of empowering people through gram or mohalla sabhas, the government says that people will quarrel. People are divided on the basis of religion and caste and therefore cannot be given any power. History is witness to the fact that whenever independence has been mentioned, people have been denied authority on the basis of the divisions that existed in society. The British also took advantage of the same. Most often, people in power do not try to bridge the divisions in society. Rather, they enlarge them so that they can cite these chasms as reasons to not vest any authority or power in the people. At times, our leaders, politicians, political parties and officers indulge in the politics of divide and rule. We need to first and foremost tell our leaders, 'We will work away our differences but we want power. You have misused the power that we gave you on 26 January 1950, and so we want it back.' The other thing we will have to do is start a campaign to eradicate segmentation in society. Therefore, it is imperative to have gram sabhas in every village.

We have to ensure that the gram sabhas don't end up like government meetings where favouritism rules the roost. The social activist, Dr B.D. Sharma, says that the gram sabha should start with a 'How are you?' For some time, people should ask after one another. People should be free to share their domestic troubles in a gram sabha. It should be the stage for discussing personal, familial, social and village-related issues. People should talk about their problems and there should be efforts to find a solution at the village level itself. For example, if someone is ill in a family, the gram sabha can discuss how to help him. This will ensure a bonding between the people. More and more people will attend the gram sabha meetings.

It is good if the sarpanch of your village is willing to convene a meeting of the gram sabha every month. But it does not matter if he is not willing to do so. You can start calling a meeting of the entire village in any particular place. Fewer people will come in the beginning. You must make an effort to call the Dalit families, for sure. Everybody should be free to air their problems and look for a solution together. Even if few problems are solved, it will result in more and more people coming for the meetings.

The pradhan should be invited for every meeting. If he does not come after two or three meetings, then, under the Right to Information Act, information about the work carried out in the previous month should be extracted and placed before the people every month. It is imperative to have transparency during meetings in every village.

Just as there should be gram sabhas in the villages, the towns should have mohalla sabhas. Get the people together. The most important thing is that people should connect with one another and there should be a social relationship. Slowly the discussion on local as well as national issues will take place. Then talk to everyone and invite the local ward councillor. Tell him about the mohalla sabha experiments being carried out in various parts of the country. Even if he is unwilling to participate, you should continue the regular meetings. You can learn a lot from the various experiments being carried out under our swaraj campaign. This is the best way to get rid of segregation and fragmentation in society. Till the politicians have the power they will only underline the differences. The day gram sabhas begin in villages and mohalla sabhas in towns, the journey to eradicate segregation will have begun.

Do tell us about your experiences with gram sabhas or mohalla sabhas by phone, emails or regular mail. We shall benefit from your experiences. If we want to change the nation, we have to work together.